I REFUSE
to Preach a Boring Sermon!

I REFUSE

to Preach a Boring Sermon!

Engaging the 21st Century Listener

Karyn L. Wiseman

THE
PILGRIM
PRESS
Cleveland

To the two people who put up with me day in and day out
as I try to be the person you believe me to be,
Cindy and Shelby.
Thanks for your love and support in all I do.

The Pilgrim Press
700 Prospect Avenue
Cleveland, Ohio 44115
thepilgrimpress.com

Library of Congress Cataloging-in-Publication Data

Wiseman, Karyn L., 1962–
    I refuse to preach a boring sermon! : engaging the 21st century
listener / Karyn L. Wiseman.
        p.   cm.
    Includes bibliographical references.
    ISBN 978-0-8298-1956-4 (alk. paper)
    1. Preaching. I. Title.
BV4211.3.W568 2013
251–dc23   2013028138

1   2   3   4   5   6   7   8   9

Contents

Acknowledgments

A book does not materialize by itself. It takes a village to write a book. In addition to my family, I want to thank my colleagues at the Lutheran Theological Seminary at Philadelphia, especially the Integrative Area, for their support and encouragement. They have pushed and pulled me along the way and have been there when I needed to vent. Words of encouragement in the halls, late night text messages, and much needed laughs were a blessing. I am honored to teach and work with you all.

I want to thank my parents, who made this possible in so many ways. When I was growing up I heard some amazing preaching from my father, Keith, and I have used one of his sermons in this book. He was a relevant, narrative preacher long before it was cool. My mother, Nancy, spent hours with me to get me caught up and on track after I was diagnosed with learning disabilities as a very young child. She was told I would never graduate from high school; my having two master's and a Ph.D. is due in large part to her efforts to redirect my path from the one that was projected for me. Thanks for making me who I am, Mom and Dad. I love you! And to my two sisters, Karla and Kim, and their families I say thanks, and I love you all. I especially want to thank my nieces, Jordyn, Jonna, Randi Brooke, and Rori, who let me tell them Fred the Duck stories for years as I honed my storytelling skills in the midst of their young lives. I am proud of the young women they have become.

I want to thank my colleagues and friends, Cheri Holdridge, Cindy Clawson, Andrea Conder, and Tommy Conder for being readers and guinea pigs for my book. They read, edited, tried ideas, and asked excellent questions to keep me moving even when I thought I was stuck. What an amazing gift as a writer to have friends and colleagues like these.

I am grateful to my mentor and friend H. Sharon Howell, who was the first woman preacher I really ever saw in the pulpit. She is my inspiration and friend, and I will forever believe her role in my life has been one of the most important ever.

I also thank the Wabash Center for the writing fellowship I received. Their financial assistance and support were extraordinary. I thank my colleagues from the best Wabash group ever for their writing boot camps and for inspiring me with their creativity and generosity.

I thank my Twitter followers, Blog readers, and Facebook friends for your words of support and for trying things out when I needed some guinea pigs out in the field.

And I thank my teaching assistant, Leah Schade, for her help in creating the "Grab Bag Sermons" exercise and for her willingness to try out some of these ideas in class. I thank all my students in my preaching classes at LTSP and at Hood Theological Seminary in Salisbury, North Carolina. These students put up with my crazy ideas and helped me grow as a preacher and as a teacher. I am forever grateful to them for this and for their love and support.

To all of the people who made this possible, I thank you from the bottom of my heart.

Opening Thoughts on Refusing to Preach a Boring Sermon

As the daughter of a United Methodist preacher, a UM preacher myself, a seminary student sometime back, a church member listening to other preachers, and a seminary preaching professor, I cannot begin to count how many sermons I have listened to, evaluated, and preached. Quite often the preaching was the center of the service, the ultimate moment of the liturgy. The preaching, however, should be only one of the moments of connection between God, the preacher, and the congregation. Preaching is very important, don't get me wrong; for preaching has been an important component of what brings us together as followers of Christ.

Preaching has the amazing ability of placing the gathered community in dialogue with the word of God, with those present or in satellite locations or—via the web—with the world around the corner and across the world—and with the preacher who has prepared the message. Throughout the history of Christian faith communities, preaching has been present. Jesus was a preacher and teacher. He learned his method of teaching and preaching from Jewish teachers and from the traditions of teaching Torah in Jewish communities. Jesus spent time talking about the Realm of God when he traveled with his disciples. He taught and preached on mountains and plains, by the sea, on boats, and in synagogues. He spoke to small groups and huge gatherings of people. He was revered, and he was ridiculed. His words had power for some and signified danger for others. People flocked to hear him and to be in his presence. He was both charismatic and profoundly personal in his relationships with his disciples and those who gathered to hear him. While we have a record of the nature of his teachings and in some cases the probable content as well, we also have a sense of how his words were received because that reception resulted in the spread of his teachings by the disciples and evangelists of his time, by written gospels and epistles written later, and by the spread of the Christian faith to virtually every corner of the globe.

But I have wondered: Did he have bad preaching days? Did some of his teaching moments fall flat on the ears of those listening? (Think about the disciples as portrayed in the Gospel of Mark.) Did some come to the mountain or by the sea to hear him and leave uninspired or disconnected? We don't know. But we do know that preachers have bad days, sermons that flop, messages that do not connect to our contexts, and listeners who are sometimes bored.

If you are a preacher, imagine the scene: you have worked for hours every day during the week doing research and making other preparations for a sermon on a text or topic you are excited to share on the coming Sunday. You have exegeted the text, studied the topic, researched several different commentaries, delved into the current context and the connections of that context to the text itself, and "wordsmithed" your manuscript or outline to near perfection.[1] You have practiced, prayed, and prepared. You have awakened early and gotten ready for the day— psychically, emotionally, vocally, etc. You feel invigorated to preach the word. You stand up, whether behind the pulpit of your church or in front of the seating area more casually, whether with a manuscript, outline, or no notes at all—and you begin to preach your prepared message.

You feel pretty good about how things are going, and you feel the Spirit in your soul as you preach. Then you look around the room and see people staring out the windows, taking a quick nap, and generally appearing uninterested. This moment has faced all preachers, whether they want to admit it or not. It can be spirit-crushing. It can be a cruel blow to one's ego as well. Working so hard on something to share with your congregation and seeing them slumbering or otherwise disconnected is tough. It hurts. You ask, "How can they be this bored?"

If you are a community member who listens to sermons, imagine this scene: you have had a very busy week at work, with your family, and taking care of home and yard. You have made the decision to attend church, gotten up, and prepared for the time in worship, either at your usual spot or in a new community of faith. You have arrived, found a parking place, and gotten yourself and your family situated for the service. You have sung the songs, participated in the liturgy, and gotten prepared for the coming message. The preacher stands to speak, and at first you are excited by what he or she is sharing. The scripture text is one you don't know very well and you are eager to hear what she has to say about the passage. But not too long into the message, you sense your mind wandering, your interest waning, and your eyes closing.

You spend more time listening to your mind read off your grocery list than you do listening to the sermon. It can be a harsh experience to feel so disconnected from the preached word. It can be disconcerting to feel bored in church. How can you be bored by God's word? How can you find a sermon based on the story of Jesus insipid? You have often been inspired, challenged, educated, and transformed by the preacher's words, but not today. As you leave you wonder, "Now what am I supposed to live on this week spiritually?" You ask yourself, "How did the preacher make this stuff so boring?"

A number of things could be going on. The thermostat in the church may be set too high, the town carnival the night before left people feeling tired and sluggish, or the sermon itself may not be connecting in ways that the preacher had hoped and planned. Perhaps the congregation was in a place leading into the preaching moment different from what the preacher thought. Maybe the preacher's preparations led to way more historical context than the sermon needed, and the people in the pews were not resonating with the information. Maybe the message did not relate well to what was going on in the lives and community of those present. Maybe it was just a bad day. Or perhaps the sermon was regrettably and unfortunately just plain boring.

No matter who you are, as you have journeyed in your faith with the church or any other configuration of faith communities, you have likely been subjected to at least a few dozen boring sermons. You have likely left a sanctuary feeling uninspired, unmotivated, and unfulfilled. You have probably sat there stumped by a preacher's words, wondering what in the world he or she was talking about. You may even have spent time hearing about the preacher's own life so much that you felt as if you had been their personal therapist for an hour a week. Maybe you have even considered sending a bill for your time as their therapist once or twice. You may have even been one of those folks catching a few zzzzzs during the sermon.

Boring and uninspiring sermons happen all the time. They come in many forms. They come in the guise of a "sermon" but may be more of a history lecture with a life lesson at the end. They may be a series of one story upon another story with little relationship one to the other. They may come as a formal "doctrinal treatise" teaching the beliefs of the church, with no way to understand the myriad theological terms used but not explained. And they may be a storytelling experience that should catch the imagination but doesn't. There are so many reasons why a congregation might hear the sermon as boring or experience the service itself as boring. How do we know? How do we keep this from happening in our work as preachers and worship leaders in a church with folks so hungry to be fed? And how do we help in the healing of folks who are just trying to survive in a hurting world?

Boring is often in the eye of the beholder and the ear of the hearer. I once heard a wonderful story about three people on a visit to the Grand Canyon in Arizona. They all happened to meet at the top of the canyon near a picturesque overlook, and they stood together gazing into the canyon. The first was an artist who admired the view and said, quite passionately, "What a beautiful sight. God has miraculously created a masterpiece that I just have to paint."

The second person was a naturalist who saw the natural environment of the canyon and its inhabitants and also saw how some of the visitors to the site had impacted the surroundings of the canyon. He said, "This is an amazing gift from God that we have to preserve and keep beautiful so that generations in the future will be able to come see its magnificence."

The third member of the group was a cowboy. He looked at the canyon and stood dejectedly shaking his head. The other two looked at him and asked, "What's wrong? Don't you find it glorious? Isn't it stunning?" "Hell, no," he said. "All I see is an absolutely horrible place to lose a cow."

I have always liked this story because it clearly displays the importance of perspective. Some gaze into the canyon and see all of its possibilities, while others see the difficulties inherent in the location. It is the same with boring experiences. Our job as preachers is to limit the possibilities of our parishioners finding what we do as boring. It is still left to their hearing of the sermon and how they perceive it, but we have to do all we can to ensure a better outcome for our listeners.

But boredom is not the only issue facing the modern preacher. One of the failures of preaching today is that too many preachers are not moving into the modern world in ways that connect to their members. Preachers are not connecting to their parishioners with the and immediacy that is much needed. Sitting in the pews on a typical Sunday, the people who come to our worship services want to hear a Word from the Lord that challenges them, that inspires them, that educates them, that engages their senses and passions, that encourages them to live more faithfully, that prepares them for the coming week, that lifts their spirits, that brings the Word into their own experiences, and that makes a difference in the way they approach their own struggles and life experiences. They want preaching that connects. They want preaching that is relevant and authentic. Many of them want more from us than they are currently receiving.

But for far too long sermons in too many worship settings have been about judgment, right doctrine, the personal experiences of the pastor, academic discourses on the exegesis of the passage to be preached on, and almost therapeutic personal musings of the clergy in charge. This does not mean that all preaching is bad. But time and time again preaching has left the folks who come to hear a message of hope and grace without that very message to take home after the service.

After all, if we do not give them something to ponder, con-sider, live on, feed on, argue about, then we are risking that those listening will find other things to do with their listening time. There is a website that lists things to do during a dull sermon, for example:

- *Missionary Pilot*—Using bulletins or attendance cards for raw materials, design, test, and modify a collection of paper airplanes.

- *Request*—Pass a note to the organist asking whether he or she plays requests.

- *Yawn*—See if a yawn really is contagious.

- *Potty Break*—Raise your hand and ask permission to go to the toilet.

- *Turn the Other Cheek*—Slap your neighbor. See if he or she turns the other cheek. If not, raise your hand and tell the pastor.

- *To Bernie or Not to Bernie*—Pass a note to someone named Bernie, but first make sure there is no one named Bernie in your congregation.

- *Liberal Church Altar Call*—If you are attending a liberal church, come forward to be "born again" toward the end of the sermon: that will really throw things into a tizzy.[2]

There are other resources with suggestions for activities during boring sermons, but many do not need such resources. When I was in high school and sat with the other young people on the back row of the sanctuary, we found plenty to do on those off days when the preaching was not at its best. We would count the times a certain word was said in the sermon; we would count the people who looked asleep; we would count the words we did not understand. Today folks have a myriad of options to keep them busy during a boring sermon: surfing the Internet on their smart phone, making a grocery list on the back of the bulletin, catching a few zzzzzzs, or texting a friend about lunch. Preachers don't need to help people perfect their "boring sermon activities" list by offering up boring sermon after boring sermon.

We have to do all we can to embrace the creativity and relevance that will give ourselves a fair chance of inspiring our listeners and being inspired as worshipers to be transformed by the preached word. To do this we must exegete the communities in which we preach; we must "pitch our tent" with them. We must learn who they are and speak out of that collaborative conversation. We must be willing to take risks and to try new things—as a preacher and as a church leader. Hans Küng reminds us that "a church that pitches its tents without constantly looking out for new horizons, which does not continually strike camp, is being untrue to its calling. . . . We must play down our longing for certainty, accept what is risky, live by improvisation, and experiment.[3] Preachers who do not pitch their tent with their church or community and do not search for new horizons cannot hope to preach engaging, relevant, and transformative sermons.

A preacher who does not risk and embrace the uncertainties of life in the midst of their context cannot hope to create sermons that avoid boredom. This is why I write about preaching. This is why I want to propose ways to connect with those to whom and with whom we share the Gospel message of Jesus Christ. And people want to connect, to be encouraged, to find hope, to hear a word of grace, and to find a community of faith to be part of. So this is the perfect time to embrace this challenge.

People today are trying to figure out what it means to be humans and to be people of faith. Talking about relevancy in preaching means we are trying to help folks understand what being human means in this context. To help people figure out the pathway to be faithful human beings in today's context means we have to make real the journey of faith in our preaching. People do not want to sit through a sermon that does not help them in this journey. Bringing "weight" to the sermon means being relevant and authentic and never boring.[4] People need to hear stories that they can connect to. As I sat with my family one Sunday in North Carolina we listened to a young preacher tell a story about her recent family camping trip in the Appalachian Mountains. She talked about the unexpected rainfall while they were putting up the tents, drenching them and all of their belongings. Laughter erupted all around us. She painted a picture of the vegetation around them and the young deer family that visited them in the early morning light. And people seemed awestruck by the image. She described the campfire and cooking s'mores over the flames, while telling stories with her children about all the times she had camped with her family while growing up in rural North Carolina. People sitting around us loved the story and were smiling and obviously reminiscing about camping in their own lives. Being outdoors is a big part of southern living and these folks were primed for her story through their own experiences.

The story connected with them with profound relevancy. Since I'm not a camper, the story did not have the same impact on me, but the community of faith that she knew and spoke to often seemed rapt by the story. And we do love s'mores, so it connected to us on some level.

People today are also crying out to belong. They want to find a community that is theirs and accepts them as part of their community. Leonard Sweet talks about "the quest for community" even in this time of individualism. Folks are not as concerned with blood connections, national identity, or similar backgrounds. They are searching for a community of choice—a group of people they choose to be part of and who choose them as well.[5]

My friend Lisa teaches children on the autism spectrum through art therapy. She took time off last year on maternity leave, and so her "kids" in the school had a different teacher. She returned hoping that some of them would remember her. During the first art exercise she got her answer. One of the children drew a rainbow and put the words "Love Dr." underneath. When Lisa asked the young girl what the words meant, she excitedly exclaimed, "I see doctors all the time, but you're the Love Dr. 'cause I remember you and you are full of love for us." What a blessing for these kids to find a place they belong and to remember that feeling so poignantly.

We have many people in the church looking for this same kind of belonging. As preachers of the gospel, as community builders, and as people of the Word it is our task to create opportunities for the people sitting in our pews, on our couches, folded into folding chairs to find in our messages an entrance into a community of faith that is rich in diversity, full of passion for ministry, driven by inspiring preaching, leading listeners into hands-on ministry, and open to the gifts of others coming into and being welcomed into community. When we preach boring or uninspiring sermons, we risk telling folks by our words and actions in the pulpit that this is not a community they want to be part of. This is an important thing for preachers to remember as we embark on a journey of learning together how to refuse to preach a boring sermon.

People today are not the same type of listeners we have had in our churches during the recent past. Today's sermon listener likely has a shorter attention span, is less biblically literate, has fewer astute critical thinking abilities, has less denominational affinity and knowledge, knows less about the church's history and liturgical traditions, and is not as clear about what they believe.[6] These are generalizations but are fairly accurate, especially for younger members, newer persons in our communities of faith, and returning folks who left the church sometime in the past. Because of this we can no longer assume a level of familiarity with biblical stories: we have to teach them. We cannot assume people understand the historic beliefs of the church; we have to teach them. We cannot use abstract stories and images to talk about faith; we have to be concrete. We cannot even assume that our preaching receives the same level of authority it once did; we have to earn it by our authenticity and relationships.

This impacts how our listeners hear what we say and how what they hear relates to their daily lives. And it should also impact how we think about preaching, how we prepare our sermons, and how we deliver our sermons, too. These developments are changing the church in significant ways. It makes sense that the church—and preaching— must adapt to these new realities. Of course, context is important, and you as the preacher have to be as familiar with your community as you possibly can so you can know who they are and what their specific needs are. God through the Holy Spirit can and will do extraordinary things with our words that we cannot even fathom. The power of the divine Spirit to use us and our preaching is profound and important, but there are also things we must do to make our preaching more

engaging and to lessen the possibilities of being boring or disconnected when we preach. Doing this honors our preaching at a
very basic level.

In this book I will look at several areas of possible growth
that all preachers can engage in to enhance their preaching, to
increase the connectedness of their words to their people, and to
avoid the possibility of preaching a boring sermon.

In chapter 1, "I Love to Tell the Story: Narrativity and Storytelling," you will be introduced, once again, to the power of storytelling and narrative preaching. People want to hear the story of
faith, the Gospel story, and the story of their own lives from the
pulpit in ways that are relevant and authentic. And they want to
hear a sermon that does not bore them. You will learn tips for telling stories, how to choose narrative pieces for your sermons, and
the importance of context. Storytelling and narrative preaching
lead us into a journey that can be profound and powerful.

In chapter 2, "Preaching and the Hokey Pokey: Enhancing
Creativity in Preaching," you will see how to learn to connect
to your inner creative self. Through exercises and engaging creativity you will have the opportunity to reach new heights in
imaginative preaching. You will learn to "play" as you work on
your sermon and will receive the amazing gift of permission
to jump into the deep end of the preaching pool (and possibly
learn to use "floaties" as some of you begin the process). Tap-
ping into your creative self can bring about new insights in both
the preparation process and the actual presentation of a more
creative sermon.

In chapter 3, "Do You See What I See? Play-Doh and Preaching," images and their role in preaching will be explored. People
think and remember in imagery, and our preaching can be
greatly enhanced by the inclusion of images as connecting points
with our listeners. You will find images in the text and in the world
to help in your preaching, and you will learn to analyze them for

possible use in your work. You will learn to utilize this powerful preaching tool, which is so pivotal to preachers today.

In chapter 4, "To Tweet or Not to Tweet: Social Media and Preaching," we will explore the roles social media can play both in preparing your sermons and in the response to your preaching. We will see how using social media technology in the preparation of your message and in the midst of your preaching can enhance your worship in profound and impactful ways.

In chapter 5, "Screens in Worship? 'Over my Dead Body' or 'Let's Do It,' " we will explore the issues involved in using visual technology in worship and in your preaching. You will learn how churches can and have engaged in creating clear reasons for using visual technology and how those decisions can benefit your congregation in the present and into the future. And I will point you to resources and needed analysis to make this kind of worship work in your congregation and within your budget.

This book is intended to bring you face to face with new trends in preaching, creative endeavors you can bring into your own process, ways to enhance your preparation for preaching and to give you some helpful tips on how to engage these suggestions. Each chapter concludes with a section titled "Things to try on your own . . ." to encourage you to practice some of the tips from this book. Encouraging you to make your preaching more engaging, more connective, more narrative, more creative, more image-rich, more social media engaged, and more technologically enhanced is a huge step into vital and more powerful preaching for the twenty-first century. Preaching boring sermons is the last thing you want to do. So I invite you to dive into the deep end, try some of these techniques, and make your preaching come alive again (or for the first time).

ONE

I Love to Tell the Story:
Narrativity and Storytelling

I grew up in Texas, where telling stories is the primary method of communication. I cannot remember a time when storytelling was not part of my life. I remember my mother telling us stories at bedtime, sometimes with a book, sometimes without, often from memory, but sometimes from the *Hubert's Bible Story Reader*. I remember my Nanny telling us stories about cooking and her life both in the kitchen as she cooked and on walks to the five-and-dime store for a treat. She was a quiet speaker, so we had to listen intently. But we never tired of her talking and telling us stories about her life. And I remember my great Aunt Edna telling us stories about the "little fairy people" who lived in the moss under her window. She made up names and histories for them and told enchanting stories that entertained my sisters and me for hours. I remember my dad telling us stories to teach us about right and wrong or about responsibility and faithfulness. Some were a bit outlandish: walking ten miles in the snow uphill both ways to school was one such gem. I remember my sisters and me making up stories about our dreams and wishes or telling each other stories about our life adventures. Some of them were embellished for dramatic effect, but they were as real as could be to us. I remember friends telling stories about their weekend activities, their dates, and their arguments with parents. Stories were a part of life. They were as constant as the Texas accents with which they were told.

I know it's true not just true for Texans. Oral culture thrives in many places, both in the United States and in other parts of the world. In many cultures, storytelling is the most important way of teaching future generations about the past. Passing on one's personal knowledge and skills and the history of one's family has often been done orally. Even expressing our frustrations about a work or family situation is usually done through story. And meeting a new person on a date usually means telling each other stories about their life and experiences; even their previous "bad" dates can be fodder for stories.

Telling stories has been part of our life journeys for as long as people have been together. You don't just sit at a table eating; you hear and tell stories. You don't just sit in the chair at the beauty parlor or barber shop; you tell and listen to stories. You don't just go on vacation; you have new experiences so you can then tell new stories. You don't just watch a movie for the actors or action; you watch them for the stories and tell others about them afterward. This is true in so many parts of our lives. Even in church. Especially in church, where we are telling the Gospel story, the greatest story ever told.

So you don't just preach a doctrinal sermon; you tell stories to help the doctrine of your sermon come to life in ways that help the people hearing them relate. Storytelling based on experiences is pivotal to the people in the pews connecting to your story. Experiential storytelling means creating space and the opportunity for all who are present to participate in the story in every possible way, especially in multisensory ways.[1] That is what we as preachers need to be doing. We need to tell a story in such a way that people see, touch, taste, smell, and hear the actors and actions in the stories in ways that bring them into the story in a participatory manner.

Think of the scene where Jesus calms the storm. Describe for your listeners the details of first-century boats, the sleeping arrangement on a hard wooden floor, the stench of humans and fish intertwined, and the smell of fear all around you. Describe the wind licking up as the storm comes closer and the waves begin to rock the boat more violently. Talk about the sea sickness beginning to overcome some on board. Describe in detail what the wind sounded like and how the boat's mast and gear were bending and banging from the storm. Talk about the hushed voices of worry turning to panicked cries of terror as the storm raged on. This is what great storytelling is all about: bringing the listeners into the story and leading them to want to see, hear, smell, feel, taste, and experience the story as they hear it told. Set the scene with vivid detail upon detail so your listeners can enter into the story on as many levels as possible.

One of the most powerful characteristics of storytelling is the act of connecting emotionally with the listeners. They come hungering, for the most part, for something to touch them. They want their inner selves to be touched by the sermon, the music, the experience. They want a connection to the Holy and to their own lived experiences. Stories allow us to touch the heart, mind, and soul of our listeners, even those who may not have come hungering. Stories allow our listeners to be engaged in ways that are more connective and personal. For preachers, relationships are key: relationships to the text, to the context, to the listeners, to the community. Getting the people to understand your heart, mind, and soul by telling stories that illustrate who you are as you share the Gospel lets them be more open to the other stories you tell. Relationships within the stories help your listeners understand their own relationships with others, with their faith journey, and with God. But stories mean different things to different people. Stories convey several perspectives, and the listeners determine how to receive them. The Holy Spirit and God's presence in the listening also greatly impact how people hear and relate to a story, but we have to do our work as well. As people listen they participate in sensory manners, with their eyes, ears, taste, smell, experience. This is a fact of storytelling that we cannot forget and must embrace both as we prepare to preach and as we engage in the actual preaching event.

All stories convey messages on a number of levels. Remember the story about the Grand Canyon in the Introduction. Some gaze into the canyon and see all of its possibilities, while others see the difficulties inherent in the location. The story can be about geography, about differing perspectives, or about the way nature is viewed by different people, among others. It is a story that can be understood by people who have seen a natural valley or strata of the earth exposed. But it can also be understood by just about anyone who has seen a photograph of the Grand Canyon or any canyon for that matter. The level of detail and perspective in a story can invite listeners to join in the telling by imagining themselves in the midst of the story or imagining the elements of the story separate from themselves. The visual clues we provide as we tell the stories give listeners more tools with which to hear and interpret what it is that they hear. Having a flow to the sermon that comes from the typical narrative story allows listeners to maintain interest.

Many writers have commented on the fact that listeners today do not have the same attention span as listeners in the past. This is a generation that has lived with a remote control in their hands, has skipped their DVRs through commercials to get to the good stuff, and has little chance of maintaining long-term attention in most circumstances. (Maybe a bit of ADHD out there?)[2] Making sure our stories make sense, flow naturally, and have an emotional connection is vital to avoid boring sermons and to keep the attention of the listeners.

Sermons are often deeply associated with storytelling. The biblical account itself is a story central to the act of proclamation. The lives of the listeners of any given sermon are important aspects of the story. The exegetical process and research of the preacher about to preach the sermon are another story. Context and story are vital to creating a sermon and a situation that connects to the lives of those who are listening to the message. Teaching theologically about our faith is often done in story form. So stories make sense.[3] And they can stay with the listener longer than a typical doctrinal or straight exegetical sermon. Remembering this is an important first step in moving your preaching forward.

An important concept in preaching with narrativity and story is the KISS metaphor: "Keep it simple, Stupid." Although I hesitate to use the word "stupid," I believe the formula is important. No matter who we are dealing with, we need to limit the ideas introduced in any given sermon.[4] This is especially true for postmoderns, but in my experience it is true for just about everyone else as well. Limiting the number of ideas introduced in a sermon gives our message clarity and keeps the focus on the particular text we are addressing. Too many preachers preach too many sermons that I would call "kitchen sink sermons"— because they have put everything in it but the kitchen sink. Adding too much is just as bad as not having enough in your sermon—maybe worse.

Another characteristic of listeners today is that they like stories told in a non-linear manner.[5] Telling a story that moves the scripture passage, topic, doctrine, or subject of the sermon forward in non-linear or in a less linear fashion keeps the people engaged in ways that a linear, dogmatic sermon typically cannot. Movies are sometimes told in chronological order, but more often these days they are less linear and more twisted in their plot lines. Lots of folks enjoy this immensely. Some use flashbacks and others use a disjointed plot line to increase the suspense and highlight the change in characters or their motivation in the story. This we can also do in preaching. Maybe you won't go as far as the 2000 movie *Memento*, one of my favorites, which tells the story of a man who can no longer build memories and is using notes left to himself to find his wife's killer. The story is told forward in some parts of the movie and backward in other parts, revealing more and more about who he is and who killed his wife. It is considered a classic of out-of-sequence movies, but not many folks could follow this type of sequencing for a sermon without the visual cues used in the movie (black and white for chronological parts of the film and color for events going back in time). But allowing our listeners glimpses of where our stories are going and then leading them back to the beginning can engender interest and pave the way for more powerful storytelling.

When I was about five years old, my father, a United Methodist preacher, told a story that I remember to this day. He did not read the text assigned for the day. He simply started telling a story about two brothers, one named "Hairy" and the other named "Grabby."[6] My dad talked about their physical attributes and told their birth story. They were fraternal twins, but evidently they were quite different from each other. The first-born was hairy at birth. The second-born came out of the womb grabbing onto the foot of his older brother. My dad talked about the ways Hairy, the first-born, grew up outdoors—hunting and fishing with his dad. He often stayed outdoors for days camping and living off the land. He was gruff and masculine and deeply loved by his father. Grabby, his younger brother, on the other hand, liked to stay indoors and cook with his mother. He was her favorite, and she spoiled him. He was a gentler man with softer hands and a personality different from that of his slightly older brother.

One day the younger brother and his mother were talking about the elderly father and his will being read soon after his death, which was fast approaching. They decided to trick both Hairy and the father into changing the will to leave all of the property to Grabby. So Grabby cooked an extraordinary pot of pork and beans, seasoned with brown sugar and cooked bacon, to tempt his brother. Hairy came in from a hunt starving, smelled the cooking in the kitchen, and was so anxious to eat the beans . . . and you know the rest of the story.[7]

I heard this story once over forty years ago, and I can still retell it. I can remember the way my dad told the story, and I can almost tell how my mind worked to figure out where the story was going. It was an extraordinary experience that I resonate with still today. The retelling of the story of Jacob and Esau as Grabby and Hairy has stuck with me because it was new and interesting. It stuck with me because it was intriguing and fun. It stuck with me because it felt like a new story. It stuck with me because it was a fantastic story. And I went home to read and reread the biblical text it was based on in my *Children's Bible* to compare dad's story to the one in Genesis. The story stuck with me because it moved me into thinking differently about the text that day. It stuck with me because it was something contextually relevant; everyone in West Texas knew about pork and beans and about hunting and fishing. And it stuck with me because this story of Jacob and Esau helped me to remember who I am and who I aspire to be. That's what stories can do for us as preachers and for our listeners.[8]

Unfortunately, not every story in every sermon will be worth remembering. After all, preachers are human. We have good days and bad ones in the pulpit. We have sermons worth remembering and some that are forgotten almost as quickly as we preach them, hence the purpose of this book. We tell some great stories, and we tell some lame ones. But our goals as preachers ought to include making connections with those who listen to us. It ought to be our deepest desire for folks to leave their pews after worship with something to challenge, engage, and affirm them in the week to come. Stories can do that in an intriguing manner.

Narrative preaching and storytelling are powerful tools of the pulpit. I have heard sermons preached that were one story after the other with no logical move from one to the next, leaving listeners wondering, "What was that all about?" I have heard sermons that contained a profound story interwoven with the biblical text in ways that brought meaning and relevancy to the message. I have heard stories in sermons that fell flat, like the story of a woman who lived in a large West Coast city who got up late and was frantically running through the streets to catch a ferry to take her to work only to discover (after jumping onto the ferry thinking she was missing it) that it was actually just coming in to dock. Okay, I admit it. I told this lame story in rural Kansas. The story itself was not necessarily lame, but telling it where I told it was. It did not fit the context of my congregation and barely fit the sermon's intent. A male member of the church said to me as he left that day, "Pastor Karyn, I didn't get your story but you sure told it as if it was funny." Wow. I was embarrassed and resolved never to do that again. If "location, location, location" is the motto of real estate, then "context, context, context" is the motto of relevant preaching for the twenty-first century.

I have heard stories in sermons that made me laugh and some that made me cry. I have heard stories that challenged the listener as well. Some stories push us out of our comfort zones. Some stories force us to confront our own prejudices or assumptions. When we tell a powerful story and that "story becomes personal and people begin to become unsettled and challenged by it, then they have been touched in a place where facts fear to tread."[9] Telling stories with various levels for our listeners is vital. Let's take the story of Jacob and Esau as an example:

> These are the descendants of Isaac, Abraham's son: Abraham was the father of Isaac, and Isaac was forty years old when he married Rebekah, daughter of Bethuel the Aramean of Paddan-aram, sister of Laban the Aramean. Isaac prayed to the Lord for his wife, because she was barren; and the Lord granted his prayer, and his wife Rebekah conceived. The children struggled together within her; and she said, "If it is to be this way, why do I live?" So she went to inquire of the Lord. And the Lord said to her,

"Two nations are in your womb,
   and two peoples born of you shall be divided;
one shall be stronger than the other,
   the elder shall serve the younger."

When her time to give birth was at hand, there were twins in her womb. The first came out red, all his body like a hairy mantle; so they named him Esau. Afterwards his brother came out, with his hand gripping Esau's heel; so he was named Jacob. Isaac was sixty years old when she bore them.

When the boys grew up, Esau was a skillful hunter, a man of the field, while Jacob was a quiet man, living in tents. Isaac loved Esau, because he was fond of game; but Rebekah loved Jacob.

Once when Jacob was cooking a stew, Esau came in from the field, and he was famished. Esau said to Jacob, "Let me eat some of that red stuff, for I am famished!" (Therefore he was called Edom.) Jacob said, "First sell me your birthright." Esau said, "I am about to die; of what use is a birthright to me?" Jacob said, "Swear to me first." So he swore to him, and sold his birthright to Jacob. Then Jacob gave Esau bread and lentil stew, and he ate and drank, and rose and went his way. Thus Esau despised his birthright.[10]

You could tell it as a straight story, just as it is told in the Bible. Using the original story you could even tell it without reading it. Tell it in the voice of one of the brothers in a first-person narrative or from the perspective of the father after learning of the deception. There are various options in this story. You could take some poetic license and change the story's time and place (as my father learned to do from his seminary professor) into the story of Hairy and Grabby in a West Texas fashion. Another option is to retell the story with the young men's mother having a "discussion" with a friend or relative concerning all that has transpired. Perhaps you could create a dialogue sermon with another person, having the voices of the two main characters talking about what happened at some point in the future. First-person narratives—preaching in the voice of one of the characters—can be quite powerful. There are numerous options for this type of narrative sermon. Play with the possibilities, and let your imagination loose. Read the text in a number of different translations to see if words or phrases jump out at you from one translation more than another. Read the text putting yourself in the position of Esau one time and then entirely change your perspective and read the text from the perspective of Jacob. Then ask yourself some important questions:

- What emotions rise to the surface when you read this story?

- Who do you relate to more personally? Why?

- What is it about the other person that you find harder to relate to?

- Which character do you believe your congregation would relate to more? Why?

- How might the story be told in your context? Where would you set the scene?

- What are some of the issues to be careful about in this particular story?

This and other stories from the Hebrew Testament and the New Testament provide many options for us if we just take the risk and try a few new ideas in the telling of them. Spending time asking these types of questions to engage the text and its multiple meanings will add depth and interest to your preaching. But cautions still remain.

As a preaching professor hearing sermons, in my visits to churches to evaluate preaching, and as a member of a community of faith hearing sermons as a worshiper, I hear a lot of happily-ever-after stories. These stories tell of overcoming trials and tribulations, conquering fears and setbacks, and turning away from addiction or bad decisions. I call these "God always wins" sermons. The problem is that the people in the pews are often left wondering, "Why didn't my mom win against her cancer?" Or "Why can't I get a job if everyone else gets past their rough times?" The "overcoming" stories serve a purpose, but often we need to trust our listeners more and let them see that things do not always work out for the best, but God is present in those situations just as much as God is present in the overcoming stories we so often tell.

Heather Murray Elkins helps us understand the importance of orality in the midst of preaching and worship:

> Orality, not literacy, shaped the early [Christian] community's perception of Word and worship. The scriptural texts read in public worship required the sound of the human voice in order to be complete. The saying of a thing was the doing as well: the physicality of an apostolic letter being unrolled and read, the experience of singing in one voice, breathing with one breath, blessing one God. This involved *perception*, the sensing, and making sense, of objects and subjects. This embodied language made a lasting impression on holy and human forms of communication.[11]

Addressing this orality is important, but the move to orality is not new in preaching. Preaching has always been an oral event, but the act of preaching has been shifting in recent decades. The move to narrative preaching extolled by Craddock, Lowry, and Buttrick in the wave of New Homiletics was a first important step to narrativity. They taught a new generation of preachers to value organic plot, to fully engage their context in the preparation of sermons, and to allow stories to make their own point instead of serving as proof of an earlier element of the sermon.[12] Today, postmoderns and virtually any persons interested in relevant preaching are pushing preachers to address the needs of a new generation of listeners and of established generations who may be tired of the same old boring and disconnected sermon from the pulpit. This type of relevant preaching is connected to real-life examples found within the experiences of those present—not some stories found on the Internet or in a sermon illustration book. This type of relevant preaching is interactive and participatory: in the sensory telling of the story, in one's asking one's own questions and coming up with one's own answers, in the fact that the listeners are allowed to have their own understandings and perspectives on the story, and in the ways the story is told—often with the help of others.

So what does a participatory story look and sound like? Imagine the preacher beginning the sermon by asking the congregation about their favorite vacation. Then the listeners are invited to journey there in their mind's eye. The preacher invites them to see the landscape they loved, to hear the waves of the ocean or the breeze blowing through the mountain trees. Next, they are invited to take a walk on a path they can visualize from their visit to this vacation spot or from another time in their lives. While they journey as a group—but also as individuals on their various paths—the preacher invites them to imagine God walking with them on this path. They are invited to talk to God about what they fear, what they celebrate, what they are worried about, what they are struggling with. In silence, the group is allowed to talk and listen to God on this journey. Some will imagine a peaceful and engaging walk and talk with God. Some will find a nice bench or rock and sit a while to talk with God. Some will be frustrated with God and how they feel God is or is not present in the ways their lives are unfolding. Some will struggle with the exercise as visions and imaginative experiences are not easy for them. If needed, the preacher can lead them in a quiet voice. But all are invited to journey in whatever way is best for them.

This is an experience connected to their personal lives and their past. It is an experience designed to move them into closer conversation and relationship with the Divine (and they are invited to envision the Divine in any way they wish). The preacher brings the group back together, gently and slowly, and helps them to debrief their experiences as a group or in dyads. This can be accomplished by using another visual imagery device that helps them imagine walking back to this place and time or asks them to reenter the present worship experience through quiet music. Either way allows some transitional time so that people are not too abruptly moved from one "place" to another. The preacher can then bring the sermon to a close by talking about the many ways and places we encounter God as we walk the journey of our lives day in and day out. This is a powerful way to invite listeners to be active participants in the message.

A different example of a participatory and interactive sermon is when the preacher starts the sermon with questions and asks for answers from the gathered community. There are a number of ways these answers can be gathered. In a sermon a few years ago, I was using a Eucharistic text and focused on the feast of the Lord. I mentioned to the group that my Nanny always told me that "where two or more Methodists are gathered, there is fried chicken." (This is likely true for most communities of faith, but this was our family's experience). I asked my listeners to tell me what their favorite potluck dishes were. And they began to call out: red Jell-O with fruit, green bean casserole, sliced ham, chocolate pie, ambrosia, and other favorite dishes they had shared at numerous potlucks in their own past. It was fun, and it made us a bit hungry. The items can be gathered verbally as the preacher calls on one person at a time to share. Or persons present can tweet or text their answers to a known receiver on the staff or church member who has agreed to serve as a moderator. These can be posted on a screen in the front of the sanctuary or sent to the preacher's device so that he or she can incorporate them into the sermon. The preacher can also solicit answers to their questions online before the sermon—via email, Facebook, Twitter, or other social media (more on social media and technology in preaching in chapters 4 and 5). These opportunities to share in both personal and more technological matters can lead folks to feel more connected to the message.

Another way to tell the story is through drama. You can rewrite the text as a dramatic reading or write it as a drama to be acted out by congregation members. Changing the way you communicate the message is vital for twenty-first-century preachers, but the timeless message of the Gospel does not change. By being creative and open to change in how we share the story, dramatically or narratively, is what is critical.[13] There are sources like *Bore No More* and *Bore No More 2*, from Group Resources, that enable you to engage your congregation in active participatory activities that range from low anxiety to high participation.

Other examples can be found elsewhere in this book. The Hokey Pokey story in the next chapter is an example of a participatory sermon. The story of Hairy and Grabby brought the listeners into a story by inviting them to imagine the story anew and with a different context, one known to them in West Texas. The idea is to involve the listeners on as many levels as possible, as often as possible. It is about creating opportunities for active participation in worship: sensually, visually, orally, spiritually, and physically.

A difficulty in moving to this type of preaching is the inherent resistance to changing the ways we preach. If you were taught to use Paul Scott Wilson's *Four Pages of the Sermon* or Eugene Lowry's *Homiletical Plot*, changing to a more narrative and participatory style might cause fear and alarm. However, the move to a more narrative method of preaching can be an enjoyable journey as well, and in many ways narrative is part of those preaching styles already. One of my favorite authors on this journey is Alyce M. McKenzie. Her work is instructive in helping the preacher to think about the written sermon as a narrative process from the outset. In her work *Novel Preaching: Tips from Top Writers on Crafting Creative Sermons*, she reminds us that we learn best from images and in interactive ways.[14]

Preaching to avoid boring our listeners and to inspire our community should address these best methods. She further pushes the preacher to create deep, spiritual, relevant, and imaginative sermons. These are the sermons that people respond to. These are the sermons that keep our listeners engaged. Our listeners need story and imagination. They need to be taught, led, and challenged. They need to be invited to "see" the sermon in vivid detail. They need to hear metaphors and analogies that are concrete and that they can relate to. They need to feel like a lot of this is coming from the midst of the community and not just from the pastor's heart and mind.[15] That's powerful and connective preaching.

My advice, along with that of many others, is to approach the task of writing a sermon as if you were approaching a work of fiction, a short story, or a novel. We have to create a plot with characters and story lines that make sense to the listeners. The plot does not have to be linear and carefully laid out but it has to be coherent. The characters do not have to be present in the room with you, but they have to be characters that those in the pews or chairs can relate to and see in their own lives. The subject of our story, our sermon, our worship service ought to be worthy of those present.[16] Too often preachers tell stories of persons that our own people cannot relate to, even on a surface level. We have to find stories and characters that our people understand, live next to, or would grab a drink with. Occasionally, we can use the overcoming hero stories to inspire, but most of the time people need to see their own lives reflected back to them in the sermons we preach, and seldom do we pastor churches filled to the brim with life-conquering heroes and heroines.

Another important method for creating narrative preaching is to write out a sermon intended to be spoken. Many preachers make the mistake of writing to read, not writing to speak. At its core, preaching is an oral event, and we have to create sermons that reflect that orality from the outset. To do this we preachers must live at the intersection of inspiration and imagination. We have to pay attention to the world around us, interactions we have with others and with the text, the various readings for the day, and our own musings, and then we should play with them as a creative endeavor with orality at its center.[17] We should go ahead and write out our sermon or outline. But then we should go back through it and rewrite it all in an oral fashion. Make it more like a script than an academic paper. Forget about perfect sentences and focus on making the sermon an oral event in every way you can.

In her book *The Write Stuff: Crafting Sermons That Capture and Convict,* Sondra Willobee gives us examples of how to write narrative sermons. She suggests that preachers use a hook to gain the listeners' attention, that we connect to our deepest imagination and theirs, that we create a relevant and cogent plot, that we find intriguing stories to tell, that we dig deep into the story of the Incarnation to help folks hear the Gospel, and that we work on refinement and revision of our sermons.[18]

To this I add that preachers should practice telling stories and practice delivering their sermon orally. Many inexperienced preachers and experienced preachers as well write just as they do for academic papers. They write "paper/sermons" intended more to be read than spoken. They get their grammar correct, make sure the theology is described in detail, make sound and cogent arguments for their point of view, and write some remarkably intricate sentences. I say these sermons are "wordsmithed" to within an inch of their life. That is all well and good for an academic paper, but it is not appropriate for sermons. We have to stop perfecting the writing and work on the connecting, the storytelling, and the relationships in preaching with more intentionality. Stop "wordsmithing."

Preachers have to throw away the habit of writing to prove an argument or writing to make a theological point without connecting that theology to the lives of those who hear their message. They have to write sermons that point to the cross. They have to write sermons to help folks on their journeys of faith. They have to write to bring people into deeper relationship with Jesus and with their Creator. Doing this takes practice, so you must work on it. Take some time to look at old sermons. Are the sentences perfect for reading—or for speaking? Read a sentence out loud. Then rephrase it in your own words and say it aloud. Which sounds more sincere? Which seems more easily understood? Which grabs your own attention more? Which would a person new to the faith connect with more easily? In my experience the one spoken with an oral syntax instead of a read syntax makes more sense. All of this takes practice and repetition to make it part of your regular sermon preparation routine.

It may seem strange that writing is such an important part of a chapter on narrative preaching and storytelling. But for many preachers, writing is the only way they know to prepare a sermon. I am one of those preachers who never writes out a manuscript when preparing for a sermon. I create a document from my research, exegesis, topical reading, news watching, and contextual analysis that is more outline than anything else. I understand the importance of preaching without notes, or as few notes as possible, in the case of narrativity. Joseph M. Webb, the author of *Preaching without Notes,* is the key voice for me and many in this work. Among the most important things Webb says about listeners and preaching is this: "Laypeople tend to believe that preachers, by and large, are not doing the best possible job that they could do in the pulpit, and that their chief failing is not theological or pastoral; it is a failure in public speaking."[19] Webb reminds us that the best way to connect with our listeners in the most intense manner is to preach without notes.

There is obviously a fear factor in moving from a written manuscript to outline or fewer notes, but in storytelling using as few notes as possible is pivotal. For one thing, the preacher who is used to manuscript preaching at the very least needs to make every effort to memorize the key story, the beginning, the repeated refrain, if used, or the end for each sermon. This allows for the listeners to see their eyes, feel their connectedness, and feel more bonded with the speaker.[20] Further, the preacher who preaches without notes provides an opportunity for listeners to participate in the sermon more fully. When listeners know, or sense, that every word is carefully formulated and preplanned, their engagement is lessened. But if the listeners sense that the words in the sermon are emerging as a spoken word event, they feel like they are part of an unfolding event and not an orchestrated or pre-planned activity.[21] Lastly, many who listen to sermons believe a message delivered without notes feels more authentic than one read from a manuscript.[22] This does not mean that manuscript preaching is less authentic; it simply means we have to be aware that our listeners sense things as we speak. To tell a profound or powerful or emotive story without notes will "feel" more connected, participatory, and authentic to the listener. These are important concepts to remember in preaching. Taking the plunge to preach either paperless or with fewer notes over a period of adjustment and change can be a powerfully liberating opportunity not just for the preacher, but for your listeners as well.

When I made the leap to preaching without notes, it was a fluke. I was serving as the pastor of LeRoy UMC, a very small rural church in eastern Kansas, and I was also the associate pastor at Burlington UMC, a five-hundred-plus membership church a few miles down the road. I wrote out a sermon one Sunday for my small church and left it on the pulpit at LeRoy ready for me to preach later in the morning. I first was to attend and assist at the 8:30 a.m. service at Burlington. I walked in and saw that my name was in the bulletin for preaching that day, when I clearly knew I was on the schedule for the following week. But the senior pastor had not prepared a sermon that week since he thought that it was my week to preach. He had nothing, nada, zilch. I had a sermon fifteen minutes away, but the service was to start in twenty minutes. So I went into the office and tried to remember as much from my sermon as possible. I jotted down the few things I knew from memory and went into the pulpit terrified. It was not the best sermon I ever preached, but it was definitely the most liberated one. I felt free to move around, make more eye contact, and be more physically connected with my listeners. I loved it.

And so did they. I got remarkable responses from them and from the senior pastor, Tom, who said, "You should preach like that all the time. You were so animated and passionate. You had the people in the palm of your hand the entire time. They were so engaged." And I went home determined to make the move to never again use a manuscript. For me, it works. It did take me a few months to find my rhythm of writing, crafting, and preaching to figure out what was the best methodology for me to use in the preparation and preaching of a paperless sermon. However, it was well worth the journey. For you, it might take another type of process. You need to try different methods and find the one that is naturally and authentically "you" in the preaching moment. You can push yourself to try new things, but you also need to know yourself.

Let me share my method. I start on Monday by reading the text in several translations and making initial notes and comments. I spend time in prayer and keep the text on my mind as I drive, exercise, or go through the day. I usually take notes on my smart phone, but you could also use a small notebook to record your thoughts and ideas. On Tuesday I do some research in commentaries and other sources. By Wednesday I have written a fairly detailed outline using my notes and thoughts from the previous few days. This means I have plenty of time to begin memorizing the flow of the sermon. I spend Thursday and Friday working on sequence and flow. I do not memorize the outline. I memorize the main elements of the arc, the trajectory, of where I am going in the sermon and the transitions from one element to the next. I also practice the story and/or the end of the sermon.

Doing this work ahead of time allows me to become so familiar with this sermon that I can give it without using the notes. The problem for many preachers is that they wait too late into the week to allow for this kind of memorization. Using my process, or someone else's process that you have found works for your weekly writing routine, preachers moving to a paperless preaching event can be helped immensely. My advice is to start slowly. Remember to memorize your major narrative piece: your story, your beginning, or your end. Work forward from there. Try memorizing these sections as you move forward. You may never get to full paperless preaching, but preaching some sections of your sermons without notes is much more connective, participatory, and authentic in the minds of the listeners.[23] Most of us have sat in a worship service and listened to preachers read a story from their own lives. I sat in a service in North Carolina several years ago and listened to a pastor read a story about her family's beach vacation that had just happened the previous week. As I sat there trying to listen, an elderly woman in front of me leaned over to her friend and said, "She can't even remember what happened to her last week. And I thought my memory was bad." The women were unimpressed with her story as she read it. They could not fathom why she read it. And neither could I. You have to be able to tell stories from memory. And practice makes perfect—practice in the car, at the dinner table, with a friend. But make the effort to practice your stories—often.

This chapter is about story and about making your sermon as narrative as you can. When you're trying to avoid any chance of bringing a boring sermon into the pulpit, story is one way to make that happen. Tell stories, be narratively focused, write to speak, not to read, and use fewer words written down on a piece of paper in front of you. These are important steps in moving into the twenty-first century: non-boring sermon territory for your task as a preacher.

Things to Try on Your Own

1. Read the text you have decided to preach about for the coming week. Read it from at least four different biblical translations. Write down any words or images that come to your mind. With this list, imagine the connections between the people in your current context and the text you are using. Draw out lines of connection to events, people, places, or other things common to your context. Make a word or image map of all the connections between images, stories, and people. Focus on this map and pray for these connections. Focus on which ones seem most relevant to your context, to the text, and to the current events.

2. Read the text for the day and spend some time retelling it in your own words, in another time period with new contextual elements (like Hairy and Grabby), or tell it again as one of the characters in the story. If the text is not a narrative text, allow the text to guide you. If it is a historical piece, retell it in another time. If it is a poetic piece, rewrite it as a poem or a song using more current contextual elements. If it is a doctrinal piece, tell it as if

you are trying to teach a very young child (using simple language and simplified theology). Use these elements to create your sermon so that all present can relate and understand what it is you are trying to say.

3. Search for a relevant story that makes sense for your context. Do not tell a story that is from a different part of the country and requires intimate knowledge of that region to be understood fully. Do not pick a story that is complicated or needs several side stories to give enough context for those present to grasp the flow of the story. Use a story that makes sense for your people. Make sure it uses language similar to what they would use in their own homes, that it has images that they would be familiar with, or it has characters that they would have a cup of coffee with in the local diner. Practice telling the story in different ways to find the best way to tell it plainly in your community of faith.

4. Practice telling the story throughout the week. Tell it to yourself as you drive (people will just think you have a hands-free device). Practice in the shower, mowing the lawn, or on your evening walk. Use your cell phone or a Flip recorder and record yourself telling the story and listen and watch for better analysis of how the story is "playing" as you tell it. Practice is something we do for almost any other skill in our lives: telling stories in sermons should be no different.

5. Memorize one or more sections and repeat them to yourself or a friend during the week. Memorize your beginning and/or ending and find ways to make them as meaningful as possible. The first words of your sermon set the tone for the listeners; the last thing they hear in your sermon is likely to stay with them longer than other

sections. Work on small pieces in the beginning. When you memorize a section, take the word-by-word sentence or paragraph out of your sermon manuscript and replace it with a key word to prompt your memory. For instance, the pastor in North Carolina could have simply had the words "Beach Story" in her notes to remind her to speak conversationally about her family's trip. This way you will not be tempted to read it. You may be able to move to an outline or only key words before you know it. If paperless preaching is not for you, you can at least memorize sections that help you connect more meaningfully with your listeners.

TWO

Preaching and the Hokey Pokey: Enhancing Creativity in Preaching

To avoid the possibility of being boring when we preach, sometimes we need to do something creative and memorable. At times sermons stick with you for just an hour or two after they are preached, and at other times they stick with you for years. Occasionally a sermon makes an impact on the preacher and on those who heard the sermon in ways that may not be known until sometime later. That is what happened to me. I was preaching a sermon in my church in Kansas City, Kansas, over a decade ago about putting all of yourself, your whole being, into the act of living out your faith and being a disciple of Jesus Christ. I spoke using several examples of persons in our community of faith who put their all into their ministry with the kids in our daycare program and in our ministry with neighborhood homeless families. I ended the sermon by asking everyone in the congregation to stand up to join in an activity with me. The congregation trusted me after five years of ministry with them so they arose in unison wondering what I was about to ask of them. I led them into a moment of absurd delight. We began to do the Hokey Pokey right there during worship—right in the pew spaces, in the center aisle, and in the middle of the aisles around the sanctuary. I had planned it. I had asked for people to serve as "plants"[1] to start it off in their sections, and I had dreamed of how well it would go.

Even a ninety-three-year-old member named Miss Nellie stood up and Hokey Pokey'd like her life depended on it. We came to the line in the song I was waiting for: "You put your *whole self* in, you take your *whole self* out, you put your *whole self* in and shake it all about. You do the hokey pokey and you turn yourself around . . . that's what it's all about!" And at that moment "ahas" went up throughout the room. They got it. It was a moment of insight and delight wrapped in a children's song that got the message of the sermon into the hearts and minds of those present.

One fifty-five-plus-year-old gentleman present that day was Dan, who had been attending our church since he was a child. He had told me on a number of occasions that he came to church out of obligation and commitment but that he struggled to have what he called a "real" relationship with God. After the service he came up to me crying. I asked if he was okay, and he asked to go into my office for a private conversation. Once there, he started crying even harder and looked at me and said, "Until today I never got that I had to put all of me into this process before it would be completely real. I had always held back a little bit out of fear and an unwillingness to go too far out on a limb." We had a remarkable talk that day and on several other occasions. From that point on he seemed to find great comfort in his new understanding of faith and personal commitment. Dan's life and work in the church changed dramatically. He was an extraordinary man, and I learned to depend on him in many ways. He was always willing to jump in and give his all to any program that needed his attention.

After I had moved away and several years had passed, I had almost forgotten about the sermon and our conversation, until I got a call informing me that that Dan had passed away. One of my former members, a member of Dan's extended family, wanted me to help with the service. Unfortunately the timing was impossible to negotiate, so I was unable to attend, but afterward they sent me a DVD of the service. And there on that DVD I saw my imagination come back to life as a letter from Dan was read. In part it said:

> For a long time in my life I was walking a road that many folks thought was a faithful one, but I was fooling myself and everyone else at the same time. I did not have a faith that was "real" until Pastor Karyn Wiseman made me do the Hokey Pokey in the middle of a church service. It changed my life. I figured out that I had to put my whole self into my faith in order to open myself up to God and to all that God intended for me and my life. And I think it might change yours, too. So today—at my funeral—we're doing something a little bit different. I invite you to join with my family and my church as we recreate that moment doing the Hokey Pokey. I'll be dancing along . . . you can count on it.   *Dan*[2]

And there in the church where I preached the sermon years earlier and where Dan "got it" for the first time, all those present for his funeral service started doing the Hokey Pokey. It was a priceless moment that touches me to this day. But the truth of the story is that it was my creative imagination and the inspiration of the Spirit that brought about that transformative event that day. It was about being in touch with my creative juices for that preaching moment to be possible. It was about knowing my congregation and their trusting me. It was about being willing to fail and to be embarrassed by something not working like I thought it would. And it was about being willing to try something new to ignite the senses of those who were going to hear and experience my sermon on that Sunday morning. But it was especially about opening up the opportunity for God to continue working on Dan in a new way, since Dan was now more understanding of his need for a deeper relationship with God and his faith.

Preaching needs creativity and imagination almost more than anything else to avoid the chance of being boring or uninspiring. Of course, preaching a sermon requires deliberate exegesis,[3] contextual study, personal prayer, meticulous preparation, careful analysis, presentation practice, and other necessary elements.

But for preaching to ignite the fires in the belly of those hearing the sermon there often needs to be something to catch their imagination, to spark their creative thoughts, and to push their minds to see where the word, the sermon, and the preacher are going. This type of creativity invites people to see a text with new eyes, to hear a story in an innovative and creative way, or to get them out of their seats to dance the Hokey Pokey.

The problem is that often, definitely not always, but all too often, preaching is too academic, unnecessarily stale, boring, and completely uncreative. This kind of preaching has led many to see preaching, and sometimes worship itself, as irrelevant and out of touch. So how do we as preachers embrace creativity to engage our own imaginations in the preaching process? I have several suggestions that have worked for me that I believe will work for you as you are working on your preaching skills.

Imagination is essential in writing, but many pastors are not adept at using their imagination in the creation of sermons. Too often preachers are focused only on the theological and biblical exegesis of the text and not on finding imaginative and relevant ways to connect these theological concepts and biblical texts to the current contexts and lived experiences of our people. Doing everything we can to increase our level of creative engagement with the text will help us avoid the boring sermon. Being in touch with our creative nature is essential in this task.

It is important to prepare a manuscript or an outline for a sermon that is theologically sound and biblically consistent. That is a given in this process. All preachers need to be attentive to these fundamental skills in sermon prep; exegesis of both the text and the context in which the sermon will be preached need to be addressed. But preachers who want to do all they can to avoid the possibility of being boring, who want to be authentic and relevant, must address the issue of creativity as well. Julia Cameron, in *The Artist's Way: A Spiritual Path to Higher Creativity,* suggests that we are all creative. All of us have some level of creativity in us. We are all gifted by the Creator to be creative. Our endeavors to tap into that creativity are our gift back to the Creator.[4] This is powerful stuff. But what exactly is creativity?

Creativity is not easily defined, and it is often defined as it is encountered. We see something we deem to be inventive and ingenious and we call it "creative." Or we see something that is not to our liking, even though it was created by another, and we evaluate that "thing" as being "not very creative." It is a value judgment. But working to engage our creativity is vital. Despite that, not all we do in creative preparation for preaching will work in all circumstances. So we make attempts, stretch the boundaries of our own creativity, and experiment to find the right balance between our creativity and the perceptions of that creativity by our listeners. It's time to walk out to the edge of the pool and jump into the deep end. It's time to stop giving our listeners a reason to be bored.

In my work with preachers, I have found that Cameron is right on point and I've seen it: everyone has some level of creativity, much of it unrealized. Some are creative in their cooking—able to take random ingredients from their pantry to make a tasty and creative dish for their supper. Some are creative in how they envision the décor of their new home when they see it empty for the first time, see it finished in their mind's eye, and find the items necessary to make that creative vision a reality. Some are painters who "see" a painting on a blank page and then use the paint to bring that vision into being. Some are gardeners who plant items in the fall that are not yet in bloom, but they see in their creative vision the final product of a lush spring garden that blooms before their eyes. Some are poets who take a multitude of words to create works of remarkable poignancy and imagination. Some are amazingly creative in finding ways to say that they aren't creative! Others are still trying to find their creative side. It takes nurturing.

And it takes courage to embrace the possibilities of creativity in one's life.

We have to discover connections to our creative selves. Ways to do this include avoiding perfectionism to allow your creative spirit the much needed room to stretch and grow; taking risks to let your creative self "play" within whatever medium you are working at the time; taking jealousy of others' talents or skills out of the equation; and finding a sacred space in which to work, a space that connects you to your creative self, to your best self, and to God,[5] You have to find that space to be creative. Maybe it means taking a walk in the woods to be inspired. Maybe it is listening to music or writing poetry. Maybe it is something else for you. The important step is that you have to figure out what you need to get into the right space to be creative—physically, theologically, inspirationally, and emotionally.

One of the keys to this is having faith in yourself to be creative, to embrace your creativity, and to connect to the divine Creator who made you to be creative. Like the Divine, there is a sense of mystery in the creative process.[6] We start with a blank page, a clean desk, an empty garden plot, or a paint-free canvas, and we go from there. The mystery of how we get from the blank page to something creative is one part God, one part us, one part mystery, one part hard work, and one part inspiration. Creating space so that you can embrace the mystery in order for creativity to flow is crucial. One of the things I do as I write or create is to give myself permission to fail, permission to be frustrated, and permission to express all of that. Sometimes I find that writing down what is not working is just as important as making abundant progress on whatever project I am working. At times just taking a break and writing down words of frustration and anger gets me moving in the right direction again. Sometimes I squeeze a stress ball to let out my frustrations. And sometimes I go see an action movie to get out my aggression. Preachers often think they must enjoy the process of writing sermons. They believe that it is a holy task and they should not ever be angry or frustrated about it. But we all get blocked at times. We all flounder in trying to figure out where to go with the text. We all fail to find the right words. We all run up against sermons that just will not let themselves be written. It is during these moments that we have to call out to the Holy and allow the divine Creator to unleash the creative spirit in us all. All of us have frustrations and blocks in our vocations. Why should preachers be any different?

So how does this work in preaching? It works much like it does in everyday life. But it also takes intentionality and practice. It is like a muscle that must be stretched, trained, and encouraged. To do this, preachers must engage in creative exercises to drive their preaching into a more creative vein and to encourage their writing process to include creativity in all they do. When you begin a new exercise routine, your muscles will be sore. You feel discombobulated and uncertain. But if you keep at it, be patient, and practice, it will become easier. It will become almost rote after a while. Your imagination and creativity muscles will get flexed and stretched so that they work in connection with your sermon prep naturally. Keep at it. Be patient. Practice.

Encourage yourself to use your imagination throughout the exegetical process of researching your sermon text or topic. To accomplish this rewrite the text as a dialogue between two characters in the story with as many details as possible, perhaps even as a script.[7] You can create a moving discussion between the older brother and the prodigal son about obligation and anger. This kind of narrative storytelling can create connections for your listeners that other preaching methods sometimes do not. Hearing the older brother rant about his work not being appreciated has potential to connect to folks in your pews in ways you would not believe. You could create a funny exchange between observers who heard Jesus tell the religious leaders about the log in their eye as they try to unpack what in the world that meant. The images alone are funny, but what about exploring the reactions of the folks hearing this for the first time? "Did you hear what he just said?" "How goofy that would look with a big log sticking out of your eye." "What a strange example he used. Where did he get that one?" Play with it a bit. The occasional use of humor regarding the biblical story is a powerful way to make it come to life for your congregation in ways they may have never experienced before, especially in church. There are often moments in the biblical text that can be handled with a sense of humor and creativity. You are allowed to take the opportunity to engage this part of who you are and what the text allows. These experiences will give your listeners new insights into the realities of life in the biblical context and how that reality relates to their own lives.

Let's look at one text from Matthew for some insights into possibilities:

> Now when Jesus heard this, he withdrew from there in a boat to a deserted place by himself. But when the crowds heard it, they followed him on foot from the towns. When he went ashore, he saw a great crowd; and he had compassion for them and cured their sick. When it was evening, the disciples came to him and said, "This is a deserted place, and the hour is now late; send the crowds away so that they may go into the villages and buy food for themselves." Jesus said to them, "They need not go away; you give them something to eat." They replied, "We have nothing here but five loaves and two fish." And he said, "Bring them here to me." Then he ordered the crowds to sit down on the grass. Taking the five loaves and the two fish, he looked up to heaven, and blessed and broke the loaves, and gave them to the disciples, and the disciples gave them to the crowds. And all ate and were filled; and they took up what was left over of the broken pieces, twelve baskets full. And those who ate were about five thousand men, besides women and children.[8]

You can create a unique and intriguing dialogue between one of the disciples and a young boy who might have provided some of the loaves and fishes for the feeding of the five thousand, even giving him a name and back story about why he came prepared for the day. I have preached this story calling him Isaac and imagining him hearing that Jesus was nearby and hurrying to get to where he could listen to this rabbi tell stories.

Maybe he wanted to see if Jesus really could heal people, because he had a parent who was ill whom he hoped to take to see Jesus later on. Perhaps this young boy was doing this "scouting" of Jesus to keep from getting his hopes up for a healing, or to keep from getting his parents' hopes up as well. Imagining and describing why the young boy came, how he prepared for the day, what his expectations were, packing up a big lunch not knowing how long he would be gone for the day, where his parents might have been, or his nervousness in approaching the disciples when they asked for food brings the story to a creative and engaging level that potentially enriches the service and the people involved. There are a number of options that could occur in this sermon. Imagining the scene, picturing the motivations of those present, putting yourself in the place of the disciples worried about the people and the lack of food, creating a scenario that moves the story forward and fills in some of the blanks. This kind of sermon can be done as a first-person narrative in the voice of the young man or as one of the disciples explaining the events of the day.

Some might be uncomfortable with moving this story in this direction. There is a long and important tradition of understanding this story as a miracle story of Jesus and only as a miracle performed by Jesus. And that is a perfectly wonderful way to address this scene. You could still preach a creative sermon relying on the same scene with a significant difference. You could also narrate a first-person narrative sermon in the voice of one of the five thousand present for the day. Create a back story for the person.

You might create a story about a grumpy man whose wife dragged him away from their home so that she can hear Jesus speak that day. As he "listens," he gets hungrier and angrier until it is impossible for him to hear Jesus. How was his wife feeling during this time? Did she ignore his grumblings and connect completely with Jesus? Play with the possibilities about other persons who might have been there and then ask some important questions of them: Why are they there? What was their intent in following Jesus that day? What did they think about the passing time and no prospect of food? What was their reaction to the miracle? Did they believe the miracle or were they searching for some other explanation of the miracle that spread through the crowd so quickly? Were they nervous about eating the food? Were they suspicious of the disciples passing around these baskets? What did they tell others when they returned home? Creating a story to tell from their perspective can help people listening to your sermon relate to their own reactions to the miracle story.

These creative endeavors from the pulpit give the listeners a break from what is typical and allow them to anticipate what might come next if you sprinkle in a variety of sermon styles and options on a regular basis. To avoid boring sermons, we should not train our listeners to expect the same thing week in and week out. We have to vary our plans, our modes of delivery, our styles, and our presentational voice to match the text, topic, or situation. We have to include first-person narrative, conversational narrative, and teaching sermons in our preaching schedule. This leads our listeners to arrive with a sense of expectation and anticipation. Isn't this what we want? Don't we want our people to arrive excited about hearing something new about the faith, about their lives, and about the Gospel of Jesus Christ? Try some variety in your preaching and you will be amazed at the response. Of course, you can also go too far and create a situation where you do things differently so often that people become a little jumpy from not knowing what to expect. Know your people and your context to get a sense of their openness and receptivity to variations. Then make decisions based on that learning.

These activities can get the preacher's mind engaged in creative imagination about what the scene looked like, what the characters felt, or what others might have seen or heard as bystanders. Writing down these exchanges may not come naturally at first for some, but practicing and trying again to engage one's imagination in the writing task will offer insights into the motivation of the characters and possible responses to situations that can enliven the preaching moment in creative ways. If writing these episodes is difficult, find a partner or friend to retell the stories to and give yourself permission to be as bold as possible, as creative as you can be, and as free with the possibilities as you can let your mind run. One of the keys is not to be afraid to sound ridiculous at first. It is only in letting yourself go that you will find your groove and your creative center.

Another writing task for preachers is to write the sermon out from the beginning as if the sermon were a novel, with setting, characters, suspense, and plot. Writing the sermon in the same vein as a novel, or short story, makes the preacher concentrate on the intricacies of the story, the flow or arc of the plot, and the feelings and intentions of the characters. Both sermons and novels create an entry point for readers and listeners to engage the story.[9] Start small if this feels daunting. Take one small section of the text or a key story you are considering using in your sermon to begin the experimenting in this way.

Preachers who create and play with stories in imaginative and engaging manners make opportunities for the Gospel Story itself to come alive. This kind of creative writing can be powerful and insightful. And it takes intentional openness to everything around you. Alyce M. McKenzie reminds us that the preacher should have "a knack for noticing" things wherever they are. Being mindful of the intriguing things that occur in the text can bring out some creative stories in the preparation of our preaching. She also suggests keeping a journal of interesting things that "float" in and out of one's mind. Doing this as the preacher thinks about, exegetes, writes, and prepares a sermon can only enhance the process.[10] I used to carry around a small notebook for ideas that came up during the day or night when I was working toward a new sermon. Today, with new technologies I use my iPad or smart phone for notetaking. This kind of easy access to "noticing notes" is powerful. Using scripture passages and intriguing moments of everyday life can also be quite relevant and connective in telling the story. It takes careful observation and intentionality to notice things. People watching, listening to NPR or other radio broadcasts in the car, watching the evening news, observing folks in a restaurant, seeing popular movies, reading the book club selection for your community, or just being more tuned into your own family can help immensely. As a preacher you should be a student of the world, a people watcher, and a full participant in life.

Additionally, in preparing a sermon the preacher should use a hook to gain the audience's attention. How you begin invites the listener into the journey of the Word. Sondra B. Willobee, in *The Write Stuff: Crafting Sermons That Capture and Convince,* suggests starting a fight (using conflict), jumping into the middle of the action, disclosing or withholding your intent, asking a great question, sketching a character, saying something striking, using an image, telling a joke (but only if appropriate), or using restraint in getting to the point, among others. It is imperative to use what is appropriate for the text, the context, the celebration of the day, etc. You have to decide how you want people to enter into the story: through a secondary character, through the eyes of the main character, through the people in the crowd, through the narrator of the story. Imagination is important; cultivating yours is vital. I always tell my preaching students to experiment, to be brave, to try on different hats, and to use different mediums of expression (e.g., art, poetry, music, creative writing, storytelling). Letting go of control is key. Preachers have to allow their minds to soar, to be creative in the Spirit, to allow their creative juices to flow freely. It is important to play with the text, language, images, and preaching style. Variety is the spice of life, and preaching is something that benefits from creativity.[11]

There is an abundance of sources for your stories. Read a lot (newspapers, blogs, online journals, books, magazines), watch movies and TV for relevancy, use stories from family (with their permission and not to embarrass them), church history (of the local church or of the larger church's story of faith), pastoral visits (selectively and honoring confidentiality), folklore and myths, art, architecture, music (hymns, pop music, raps, carols), and videos (GodTube, YouTube, and others).[12]

One of the best ways to embrace creativity is to write— often. You should write a journal, write nonsense, write short stories, write down memories, write a blog, write poetry, write anything and everything you can. You should keep your thoughts in written or digital formats so that you do not lose track of them.[13] Many digital Bibles on smart phones have notetaking capabilities that you can use to make notes connected to the text you are working on. Do this to keep your writing fresh and your mind engaged in the practice of writing. To write and rewrite is to embrace the creativity that God has placed within us. God has created you and because of this creation you too are a creative being.[14] To make this practice part of your sermon prep provides you with a stepping stone to creativity in all of your preaching. Activities that I have found quite successful in helping to embrace creativity involve rewriting a parable or gospel narrative in a current setting; rewriting a story from Christ's life as a children's story; using simple language and concepts a child can understand; rewriting a psalm in modern language or as a rap song; rewriting a prophetic text from the Hebrew Bible text as a morality fable. These are just examples; you can tap into your own creativity to come up with your own. In my own teaching, I have found these activities bring out interesting ideas, dynamic images, and inspiring vivid language, and can sometimes be shocking, insightful, and often surprising.

Some preachers have placed the characters in interesting situations—like placing the story of Jesus overturning the tables in the temple at a Wall Street bank executives' meeting or placing the story of Jonah in the midst of the current Middle East crisis or writing a rap song about violence evoking a Hebrew Bible text. These creative writing exercises push the boundaries of comfort for some, and for others the poetic license they are given taps into unknown reservoirs of creativity and imagination.

It is important to generate opportunities for creativity in the early decision making processes of our preaching. Many preachers get into habits of exegetical process from which they rarely deviate. They can get in a rut, always doing the same old routine in their sermon prep because that is how they have always done it. In forming new habits it is important to keep those patterns from emerging too rigidly. While utilizing a sermon preparation process that you can latch onto for security in your early days of preaching, it is also important to allow options for flexibility as you engage in new ways to avoid boring sermons and as you try to move your preaching forward.

One exercise I have used to move students and colleagues to be flexible is "The Two-Minute Grab Bag Sermon" (sample texts are located at the end of the chapter). On slips of paper in a bag I have noted preselected parables, Gospel narratives, and other short, familiar texts full of imagery and meaning. The preachers come forward one at a time to draw a text out of the bag. They then have thirty seconds after reading the text to prepare and then present a two-minute mini-sermon in front of the class. The preachers are required to think on their feet, to embrace their already established knowledge base of the text, to rely on their theological understandings, and to create a moment that engages the rest of those present. It is an excellent exercise to remind preachers of the need to be ready at any moment to preach and to be open to the movement of the Spirit in their preparation. I have never had anyone draw a complete blank during this exercise. They have all come up with something meaningful to share, and many have done an extraordinary job. The practice is also a wonderful way to spark ideas for the week-to-week preacher. Any preacher can take the text for the week—whether it is Lectionary-based or topical—and let their mind run wild by performing a two-minute "riff" on the text to prime their creative pump. You can do this with a study group, in your office, or even while driving around the city on your weekly errands.

Another exercise that helps spark the exegetical process is for preachers to practice their sermons with a preaching partner. I assign each student in my classes a preaching partner for the semester. Each sermon that a student preaches in class has been read and discussed with a preaching partner prior to the sermon ever being preached in class or elsewhere. The sermon has also been practiced with the preaching partner. The preaching partners are then asked to answer a series of questions about the sermon as their partner does a practice run.

- Could you sense a framework or structure in the sermon?

- What worked and what did not work as well in the sermon?

- How well did the sermon move from one section to the next?

- Did the sermon speak to your heart and soul as a message of the Gospel?

- Were you able to hear the sermon and were the gestures used effective or distracting?

- What stuck with you after the sermon?

- What were the most meaningful and lasting images in the sermon?

- Did anything distract you or cause you to become disconnected from the sermon?

- What do you wish you had heard more about in the sermon?

- Overall, what did you think of the sermon?

You might want to find a preaching partner in your denomination or in your community, maybe even in your sermon study group. Or you can record your practice sermon and evaluate it yourself; however, it is usually better to have another person or two to help in this process since they are less likely to be as personally invested in the sermon's creation as you should be.

But here's the rub: many preachers do not practice their sermons, partly because they wait too late in the week to prepare their sermons, and partly because they have felt more confident and believe they have the task "mastered" to some extent. Many preachers in the past spent hours rehearsing their sermons. I remember my father, a United Methodist pastor for more than fifty years, going over to the sanctuary to rehearse his sermon. He would often be gone for some time, and on occasion I would go with him to watch him prepare. As I entered ministry myself later in life, I spent little time practicing my sermons in the sanctuary. I am not sure why that choice, or lack of intentional choice, was made in the early years of my preaching career. But I would read over the sermons a number of times to familiarize myself with the delivery. This was an important process, but spending time in formal practice was not part of my regular process of sermon prep.

Even though I have moved from manuscript preaching to preaching without notes, careful preparation is still a very important part of my preaching process. This move caused me to practice on a more regular basis, which has helped me immensely. Today I do not practice formally, but I do go over an outline in my head several times. I practice it informally in my car, in my office, as I walk around the neighborhood, and sometimes in the shower. I have learned that I need to practice any stories I am using so that I know them as well as I possibly can. Encouraging yourself to keep practice as a vital part of your preaching process will also encourage you to make this part of your weekly regimen. You need to know how best you work in preparing to deliver a sermon, but I believe that practice and analysis of your sermon will help you make significant progress in your preaching.

You can use different types of exegetical exercises and preaching practices to enhance creativity and imagination. You can use your exegetical notes to create a rap song of historical and cultural findings or find hymn lyrics that match the images and stories you are using.

Doing the Hokey Pokey was my way of engaging the creativity of the moment, the relationship I had with the community of faith, and the texts for that particular week. As you prepare your sermons, think about ways to creatively engage your community in activities that connect them to God, to each other, and to their lives. On baptismal remembrance Sundays we often invite members to approach the font and touch the water to remember our baptism in a physical and spiritual manner. Other acts of "ritual" engagement (e.g., remembrance, centering). can also have profound impact on the ways our community of faith encounters the word and then makes it part of their experience. One example is to spend time around an image—like the journey of faith.

As a concluding ritual you could have folks come forward to receive a blessing for their journey and a piece cut from a map to carry with them in their wallet or purse to remind them that we are all journeying together and are never alone. Addressing the need to move through the barriers in our lives in constructive ways, you might preach on removing the fences that keep us barricaded. One communal ritual or activity could be to remove, piece by piece, a small fence you have used as a focus point near the front of the sanctuary. Touching small stones, candle lighting, visiting prayer walls, engaging in artistic expressions can be evocative and empowering ways to merge the word with the embodied nature of our creativity. Utilize the space you are worshipping in, find opportunities for movement and ritual, and play with the images in your sermon to find ways to have your community of faith be part of the meaning making as they engage in creative activities before, during, or after the "sermon." This expands our understanding of preaching and participatory worship in exciting ways.

In closing this chapter, I think it is essential that we as preachers embrace all that we are as creative beings in the process of researching, writing, and preaching sermons. God has created us and regardless of our doubts about our creativity, we are creatures of a creative God, and we have been gifted with that same creativity. We simply have to tap into that creativity and make it part of our sermon preparation process. Our congregants deserve this, our own call as whole beings requires this, and the Gospel of Jesus Christ offers the infinite possibilities for us to do so.

Two-Minute Grab Bag Sermon Passages[15]

Matthew 6:19–21	Concerning Treasures
Matthew 15:32–39	Feeding the Four Thousand
Matthew 23:37–39	The Lament over Jerusalem
Matthew 26:6–13	The Anointing at Bethany
Mark 4:30–32	The Parable of the Mustard Seed
Mark 7:31–37	Jesus Cures a Deaf Man
Mark 11:20–25	The Lesson from the Withered Fig Tree
Mark 13:24–27	The Coming of the Son of Man

Luke 3:3–6	John the Baptist
Luke 8:4–8	The Parable of the Sower
Luke 11:33–36	The Light of the Body
Luke 19:45–48	Jesus Cleanses the Temple
John 10:1–6	Jesus the Good Shepherd
John 15:1–11	Jesus the True Vine
John 20:24–29	Jesus and Thomas
John 21:15–17	Jesus and Peter

Things to Try on Your Own

1. Take one of the passages from the Two-Minute Grab Bag and make up a mini-sermon on the spot. Do it in your office or in the sanctuary away from the pulpit. You can record your efforts to evaluate how you do. Be creative, stretch your imagination, and try something new. Do not be afraid. See where your mind and your imagination can take you. Be bold.

2. Read the texts for the day and focus on one image, word, or phrase from the reading. Take one character and draw a picture of how you see that character in your mind—either literally or more loosely related. Write out a short story about the character's life or how the character is involved in this text. See how far your mind and imagination will take you. Set your creativity free. Do not be afraid of what comes out and do not censure yourself or judge your artistic abilities. The image is the focus. After creating this image or life story, determine how you might share this type of personal image or personality connection with your listeners. Can you describe the scene? Is it universal or more particular?

Is it something you could recreate using images from a Web-based site like Flickr, which has a search criterion for Creative Common Images that are available for use without copyright issues.[16]

3. Take time every day—or at least three days a week—to write. Even if it is only for ten or twenty minutes—take that time to write. Write short stories, write about the events of your day in a journal, write poetry, write notes about your faith journey, write gibberish if that is all you come up with, jot down thoughts about your upcoming sermons, or something else altogether. Just write something every day. Writing is a muscle and it works on muscle memory. The more you push it, stretch it, and exercise it, the better it will be when you need it for the long haul.

4. Do a character study of a major or minor character from the week's texts or a story you are considering using in your upcoming sermon. What does their story tell us about the character? What kinds of details must we try to fill in? What role does the character play in furthering the story? Can the character's story be our story? Could the character's story be told from a first-person narrative perspective? If the person were alive today, what might the person's job be? Social status? Position in the church? How does the character's faith or lack of faith teach us something new or something about ourselves? Ask many questions of this person, experiences, and the role in the story. The answers can help you gain deeper insights into their story to make it our story as a community of faith.

5. Take your notes from your exegetical research and write a song. Use any type of music that you enjoy and that

your congregation enjoys. Or find a song that matches the themes of the text. I did a sermon series in rural Kansas using Garth Brooks songs; it was the hit of the county because I used music they knew (and it was during the height of Brooks's popularity). I used "The Dance," "We Shall Be Free," and "Unanswered Prayers" over a three night revival series. I would not do the same series today or in an urban context. But it worked then and it worked there. You need to know your context. Perhaps contemporary Christian music would work in your context. Maybe pop songs could work as well. You could use U2, Lady Gaga, Pink, or other performers to help folks understand the point you are trying to get across to them. Be creative and try new things.

THREE

Do You See What I See?
Play-Doh and Preaching

Along with narrativity and story, vivid imagery is important in our culture and in twenty-first-century preaching. When my nieces were very young, I used to try to get them to go to sleep by reading them a children's book. It never worked. They knew that Aunt Karyn as the "babysitter" would end up giggling with them when they would push their heads between me and the book. They really wanted me to lie in bed with them, but if I did that, I learned, they would never get to sleep. But they still wanted to be engaged with a great story. So I made up a world and a character that they came to love, a young duckling named Fred the Duck (I know the name is kind of boring but they loved him). I made up a whole community, where Fred lived, played, went to school, struggled with his siblings, got in trouble, traveled with friends, and had fun adventures.

When I began, I was just making the stories up on the fly. They wanted a story, and I had fun creating the images of a place and descriptions of characters that I thought the girls could relate to (Jordyn and Jonna, my eldest nieces at first, and later we added Randi Brooke and Rori). I described what Fred looked like. I gave him a distinctive voice and characteristics. I described his friends—Harriet the Hedgehog, Billy the Frog, James the Fox, Sammy the Squirrel, and Mildred the Mallard. Each had an accent, a distinctive voice, a physical description, and a fun personality. Fred had parents, but I never gave them names—just voices and characteristics—because the story was about Fred the Duck and his friends. The focus was on the young "kids" in the story.

The adventures sometimes mirrored things my nieces and I had done that day; sometimes they were lessons to help the girls understand why things were happening in their lives. I described the hollow where Fred and his friends all lived in such detail that my nieces could draw it on paper and be pretty close to what I envisioned. Fred and his friends had great adventures, flying to see new sights, struggling with new skills, doing homework while wishing they were playing, learning a lesson after stealing something from a store, or dealing with family issues.

It got to the point that several times when we weren't together the girls would call and have me do a Fred the Duck story on the phone. These stories were intricate and detailed, but they were also participatory. The girls would choose which characters got to be included in each story, and they made sound effects and physical gestures for the adventures. They often would help with the accents and voices of the characters as well. Sometimes the sounds coming out of their rooms would wake the dead—or at the very least bring their parents pleading for some calm. It was a family tradition. When my own son, Shelby, was born, I also told him Fred the Duck stories. They became a part of our nightly routine. They made him happy and brought back to life a character I loved deeply. I cannot remember a family gathering when my mother has not asked if I am ever going to type them all up and get them published. The girls even went to a local park once, found a duck, took pictures, and had a huge framed print made up with an inscription on it for me as a Christmas gift. Fred the Duck has been part of our lives for almost thirty years. And everyone in the family knows what Fred looks like and what his home would look like if they saw it while out on a walk.

What made Fred the Duck so important? Probably a big part of it was that their favorite aunt was lying down with them and telling them a fun story, which was getting them ready for bed not quite as quickly as their parents had hoped. Part of it was the nature of the stories, in that they related so clearly with the lives of the girls. We even had a character whose parents were splitting up during a similar time in my eldest nieces' own lives. But my guess, and it is backed up by conversations with my nieces, is the vivid imagery I used to tell the stories. They could see Fred and his friends. They knew what he looked like. They knew what his room looked like and how his house sat by the pond. They could visualize the play area the friends utilized every day after school. They could see the plane, bike, or boat he was on with his friends on one of their adventures because I took the time and care to paint word pictures with them of the characters and the things they interacted with. The power of imagery is profound.

Our culture is rich with imagery. People see the "Golden Arches" from a great distance while traveling by car along an interstate in the United States or elsewhere and they automatically know a McDonald's restaurant is coming up on the horizon. My son could spot one several miles away. It was an extraordinary skill. The yellow-gold arch was a sign that familiar food and a play place were coming soon. He would get excited as soon as he saw them. View a magazine ad with a simple apple image with a small bite out of it and most will immediately know that it is the logo of Apple Computers.

You barely have to think when you see stop or yield signs on the road because the imagery is so ingrained in us as drivers or passengers. We remember in images. Ask anyone about their favorite vacation and inevitably they will use images and descriptive visual language to tell the story of their trip—about what they saw and the beauty of the scenery they experienced. Images are important to people. Homes are decorated with images of family members or recent trips. People talk about significant historical and family events in their lives by describing the details of the event visually. That's how we connect to their stories.

Concrete images need to be used in preaching as often as possible. Abstract images will often leave people confused and wondering what you are talking about. But a concrete image,[1] well described with powerful and vivid descriptive language, can paint a word picture that all in the room can imagine on their own—and add to in their own thought processes. The power is in the concreteness of the images. I recently went to Niagara Falls with my family for a brief vacation. I had seen pictures of the falls most of my life. I knew what to expect because of these images. Others told me about their experiences at the falls. They described the power and majesty of the water. They described the rainbows that appear in the mist of the falls. They described the view in epic visual language. I knew what to expect, but even the descriptions were not enough compared to what I experienced the first time I saw Niagara Falls for myself and we rode the *Maid of the Mist* into the falls. Those were experiences beyond compare. But the imagery of Niagara Falls was already known to me. I could experience some level of the power and majesty when someone described it for me. You can paint vivid scenes for your listeners with image-rich language that helps them to experience more deeply the sermon as you preach it.

Many pericopes for preaching have extraordinary imagery within them. Interesting and dynamic images from the New Testament include Jesus walking on the water; the image of the water jar left by the Samaritan woman at the well when she ran to tell others of her experience with Jesus; and the simple, yet complex, tiny mustard seed of faith, to name only a few. Images from the Hebrew text are just as profound and powerful; for instance, Moses striking the rock, God as a mother hen, and the Israelite army marching around the city walls of Jericho seven times. These and other images spring to our minds as we read the Bible, and the act of deliberately processing these images can add to the preacher's understanding of how the congregants might visualize what they are speaking about. Since these images already have such profound impacts as they are read, sticking with them and nurturing the imagery is essential in creative preaching.

Images can add much to the sermon's efficacy. Images have been used throughout the history of worship and preaching to great effect. Luther described the use of visual images as "The Painted Word." Throughout Christian history images have been used to teach, to edify, to inspire, to remember, and to proclaim—among other things. Images in the early church however were controversial since the Second Commandment warned against the worship of idols. This kept any images related to God from emerging in the early church and beyond in many places.

By the third century, however, images began to develop as appropriate artistic expressions. Art appeared in house churches and catacombs. *Dura Europas* from the third century is one example. There is visual evidence of a baptismal image depicted on the wall near a tub that was likely used for baptisms in this early church space. Images of Christ, such as the Chi Ro, which became known as the monogram of Christ, began to be seen in the catacombs . After Constantine, art in the church flourished in the form of frescoes and mosaics.[2] In many places, images guided worshippers to private gathering places when such gatherings were forbidden.

The medieval church was dominated by paintings, icons, sculptures, and other art pieces. After the Reformation there was great debate about the use of artistic expressions in the church. Some wings of the Reformation destroyed or removed all art from their church buildings while others felt that the imbalance of art and spirituality, extravagance and piety, had to be rectified, but not violently.

There were two iconoclastic movements in the life of the church—the eighth and nineth centuries in the Eastern Church and the Reformation in the West. Karlstadt, Zwingli, Calvin, and other Reformation leaders smashed or influenced others to smash religious art in churches throughout the West. This led to an elitism of the Word that continues to exist today in some respects. Luther argued against these practices. He cited the Second Commandment and explained that it was the "worship" of images not the images themselves that were forbidden by Mosaic Law. Luther even used art in the Bible he published in 1522.[3] This use of imagery has continued to expand into our cultural ethos. Today people are often more in tune with images than they are with the written word.

> It seems that for contemporary Americans images are replacing texts in the ability to capture the imagination and to shape worldviews. Video images, movies, MTV-like programming, television in general, video games, interactive computer technologies have captured the popular, intellectual, and religious imagination of Americans as books no longer do. Perhaps this is a comment on the postmodern context of our age: visual images are replacing written texts as the conveyors of information and meaning.[4]

Images help congregations engage their multisensory selves and allow for preaching to become even more real for those for whom imagery is an important part of their lives. If images are indeed replacing written texts then we, as preachers of the Word, have to pay attention. We have to remember that we are preaching to a people today, young and old, male and female, techies and not, who are the most visually sophisticated people in history.[5] We must address this in our preparation and in our preaching. One of the other important elements to remember is that Scripture speaks to different people in different ways. So too, images will speak to some people in a different way than they speak to others.

Analyzing images from popular media and elsewhere for inclusion in the preaching event for possible responses is an essential task. Taking the time for careful analysis is essential. This practice can create successful "preaching with images strategies" that allow congregations to see that the Bible, the church, worship, and our preaching can provide them with a new and different perspective on media (even though that might not be what we are trying to do at all). [6]

One of the best skills for preachers to develop is editing. Often deciding what to leave out of a sermon is more important that deciding what to keep in. Remember to avoid those "kitchen sink" sermons. So how do we do this? Checking what images convey is essential. Where did you find the image? Is it from a source your listeners will understand and relate to? Is the image inclusive in the ways your community of faith is? Does the image make sense with the text you are using? Can the image be described effectively and concretely? Does it speak to people of different experience levels? Can it be used legally as a bulletin cover or electronically or is it copyright protected? (If it is you should edit it out; see chapter 2, note 16.) Do the work to analyze the images for the best possible usage in your sermon. Using images will get easier as you practice. One thing you can do is look at images online (using a Google image search, Flickr, or some other photo sharing site) for images to include in upcoming sermons. If you do seasonal or quarterly planning for worship and preaching, you can do image work when you do your planning. You may not end up using the images you originally chose, but taking time to think of images as you plan will keep you focused on ways to describe and concretize, or make real, for your listeners what it is you are trying to say.

But not all preachers are tapped into their own ability to develop images from the texts or to incorporate imagery in their preaching. Creating these skills is important for preaching. When you use vague and nondescript language you have missed a great opportunity "to paint the mental picture that is necessary in order for the listener to identify with the story."[7] The key is taking the text and finding the core images both within the story itself, from the context of the time and place of the text's writing, and in the context of those who will listen to the sermon on that text.

Let's take one text as an example. Luke 13 provides us with the Parable of the Fig Tree. We read:

> At that very time there were some present who told him about the Galileans whose blood Pilate had mingled with their sacrifices. He asked them, "Do you think that because these Galileans suffered in this way they were worse sinners than all other Galileans? No, I tell you; but unless you repent, you will all perish as they did. Or those eighteen who were killed when the tower of Siloam fell on them—do you think that they were worse offenders than all the others living in Jerusalem? No, I tell you; but unless you repent, you will all perish just as they did."
>
> Then he told this parable: "A man had a fig tree planted in his vineyard; and he came looking for fruit on it and found none. So he said to the gardener, 'See here! For three years I have come looking for fruit on this fig tree, and still I find none. Cut it down! Why should it be wasting the soil?' He replied, 'Sir, let it alone for one more year, until I dig around it and put manure on it. If it bears fruit next year, well and good; but if not, you can cut it down.' "[8]

As the preacher reads this text, especially the section about the fig tree, there are several images that immediately come to mind:

- The tree without any fruit on it
- The vineyard itself and possibly other trees (with or without fruit)
- The gardener who cared for the vineyard
- Tools used to tend the soil around the tree

- ◆ Fertilizer to help it grow

- ◆ Possibly an ax for cutting down the tree

- ◆ Anticipation of waiting a year to see what happens (what does waiting look like?)

- ◆ Any others that come to your mind

As a preacher I have to determine if any of these images jump out at me as I read the text or if one or more intrigue me enough to work with them to shape the sermon's focus. Are they concrete or abstract images? Do they work in my context? Will my community relate to the image or idea? If none of the above suggestions are calling for your attention, read the text in multiple translations to see if another word or image does rise to the surface calling for more attention.

For me, there are several possibilities, but let's look at the fertilizer image. Who has not planted something, even if it was a little flower in Sunday school for Mother's Day, and had to give the planting some kind of nourishment? Maybe it was a plant feeding spike or some kind of treated soil in the initial planting. Who has not walked through a park or their college campus right after spring planting and not smelled the wafting scent of manure in the ground covering? Who has not put their hands into a fertilizer bag to spread the fertilizer over the area where flowers or fresh vegetables are planted? If you haven't, imagine putting your hands into manure. Imagine smelling the scent of fresh poo all around you. It is amazing because it signals growth and new life despite its unique and pungent aroma. And at the very same time, it is gross. "It's yucky," as most children would attest. It is not pleasant. But it's necessary for growth. We humans have to grow as well. And our own growth is sometimes sprinkled with a bit of "crap." We go through tough times, stinky situations, and, hopefully, we come out on the other side having learned something from these experiences and even from the crap we suffered through. Sometimes we even say we came out of these situations "smelling like a rose."

How many other images can you come up with related to fertilizer or growth? What must God think of us as we are provided nourishment and still refuse to grow? Thank goodness we are given more time to come through with some form of growth. But if we read the text as one of expectation of repenting and flourishing, there does appear to be a limit on how long the vineyard owner will wait before chopping down the fig tree. Is there a limit on how long God will wait for us to repent and come into relationship with Jesus the Christ? For me, the answer is no. God will continue to come back again and again to check on us, invite us, and tend us. So what do we do with this image?

Perhaps you want to address the need for our repentance to avoid being cuttings on the the vineyard floor. The imagery you evoke can be powerful, but it also can be disheartening to those who already feel as if they are not living worthy lives. I have heard this passage preached as divine judgment that results in severe punishment for those who refuse to bear fruit or repent of their sins. This image of not bearing fruit and being cut away from God, the owner of the vineyard, should be treated with great caution, but in some contexts you might feel the need to get your people to hear a word of warning. But I suggest that you end with a word of grace and a way forward for your listeners.

Learning how to utilize imagery is important for the preacher. Paintings, drawings, sculptures, and forms of artistic expression are other ways that people connect to story and text. Using art to examine the many levels of the text is an excellent way to open yourself to the possibilities of the text. To engage my students with the use of images for preaching, I have employed assignments to help them learn the importance of analysis of these images. These exercises related to imagery have had remarkable results, and many are connected to art in one way or another. One exercise I want you to undertake is to select a text (an assigned sermon text or just one you are intrigued by) and draw a picture of an image that comes to mind while reading that text.

In class each semester, I hand out drawing paper and crayons and ask my students to let their imagination run wild. The student groups in my classes are usually made up of people who are abstract in their drawing and those who are concrete. (This might be true of your study group as well.) The students' images are often deeply emotional and impactful. I am constantly surprised by the range of imagery that comes out of this activity. You too can take some paper (colored or white) and a box of crayons[9] and see what comes from your reading of the text. Here are some clear rules that I always give to my students before this exercise:

- Stick figures are artistic.

- Any image that comes to you is appropriate if it is connected to the text and context.

- There is no judgment of anyone's artistic abilities (including your own).

- Do not censure yourself.

- Let your mind run free and allow your creative juices to flow.

- Be willing to laugh and have fun while doing this exercise.

An atmosphere of openness and freedom should allow you to explore all the images that pop into your mind when you are reading the text. You can make more than one drawing, and you can even ask others to draw what comes to them as well, either in a study group or in your family. These images are clues to what is important in the passage and what will work better as an image-driven piece in the sermon. Paying attention to what can be "drawn" from the text is vital in how you approach your sermon preparation. Listen to music as you draw or take a walk in the woods to contemplate the text before you start drawing.

Do whatever it takes to engage your creativity. It may take some time, intentionality, and patience to nurture your creativity in the preparation and preaching of sermons. You will get better if you keep at it and give yourself permission both to succeed and to fail in the task. Do not give in or give up.

You can invite your congregation into this activity by leaving drawing space in the bulletins and providing pens or pencils in the pew. You can draw attention to the activity by inviting them to doodle or by having a statement in your bulletin saying that your community of faith loves art and wants you to be engaged in it if you wish by using the space in the bulletin.

On other occasions I have used an exercise that includes Play-Doh or modeling clay. Preachers are asked to read a text from an assortment I supply to the group. Then they are asked to mold something that came to mind from the text. Many of the passages have included clear images of trees, boats, bread, and other obvious concrete and visual items—but not all. Some students molded items that were not as obvious, many of which sparked wonderful conversation within the gathered group. You can engage in creative play with the text by keeping a few containers of Play-doh near your writing desk. They are inexpensive and easy to find. After you have spent some time reading (again from several translations) and meditating on your text, let your imagination run wild by getting the Play-Doh out and seeing what image or item emerges from your creative play.

Sometimes just playing with the Play-Doh or modeling clay in your hands can relax you enough for new ideas to emerge. You may be surprised by what your mind creates with your hands or what your hands create when you let your mind wander and your hands hang loose. This exercise can sometimes stretch preachers, since many have not engaged in creative "play" for some time, especially regarding sermon preparation. Additionally, many will find the exercise hard to get into if they fear artistic endeavors of any kind. Giving yourself permission is important. Keeping at it is key. Don't give up if at first your creations seem less than you would wish them to be. Remember—no judgment. Playing with words, images, crayons, Play-Doh, characters, plot, etc. are among primary tasks if we want to avoid the possibility of a boring sermon on our horizon.

Another exercise I use in class requires the students to work on critiquing images. For each sermon you should choose two or three images that might be used on a bulletin cover or on an overhead screen to augment the sermon's imagery. These images can be evaluated by providing an explanation of how you would utilize the image in your services. Adding this layer of imagery searches and analysis to your typical sermon preparation will prove to be very beneficial. Many times preachers and students in my classes have changed their sermons completely or reconfigured their sermons to build on their message's impact when images are used. Many preachers will need to address these issues since they pastor congregations that use visual media in their worship services. More and more congregations are adding technology to their worship spaces to enable the sharing of visual images and social media (more in chapters 4 and 5 on this subject). Some pastors have worship planning committees that help with these responsibilities while others will do the work themselves. The task of determining and evaluating images for preaching requires the preachers to expand their options in understanding the text's layers and how the images relate to their congregational context.

You can also take advantage of the artistic abilities of your church community during the worship service itself. I have been present on several occasions when a preacher was preaching a sermon and an artist was creating a work of art based on the text or subject as the sermon was preached. It was profoundly powerful. I want to try it myself someday. Some emergent communities are providing art stations in the worship space so that persons who wish to express themselves through art as worship progresses have an outlet to do that. Other pastors visit Sunday school classes and have children do artwork related to that Sunday's worship. The artwork can be hung around the room to engage the senses of all those present. (And it makes children and their parents happy to be included in the space.) You can also utilize the resources of your faith community and the local area to borrow works of art for a special service theme or for a season. Art and images are powerful reminders of the Divine in all of us and add much to the worship and preaching life of a congregation.

Images are an increasingly important part of the preacher's work in sermon preparation. Using your words to paint powerful images can bring people into a deeper understanding. One of my parents' former preachers, Jim Jackson, tells a story about toast that always reminds me of both a powerful image and a profound lesson. His aunt was a schoolteacher who was teaching her students about the importance of helping their parents with household chores. Each student was asked to share what they did to help their parents. One student answered, "I scrape the toast." Someone in his family was in the habit of burning the toast on a regular basis, and this child assumed the responsibility for scraping off the burned places. Family taking care of each other, someone helping with the rough spots in life, making a way through difficult times, and other lessons can be taught from this story.

People in your congregation will likely be able to relate to this story on a number of levels. Some will simply relate the story to the breakfast they had earlier that morning. Some will relate it to the chores their parents forced on them or that they are battling with their kids to complete. Others will laugh at the burned toast image knowing that is often how theirs ends up as well. And still others will feel the intense responsibility of doing their part in the family during tough times, making the way easier for someone they care about or loving someone so deeply you would even scrape toast to show you care. Considering the possibilities of how listeners will hear this story is important.

As preachers we can utilize images like the burnt toast and others to remind, challenge, encourage, teach, illuminate, and inspire our congregations. Paying close attention to this task, playing with imagery, stoking the creative fires around imagery, and utilizing all the possibilities for visual aids (moving pictures, still images, etc.) are an increasingly important element of the preacher's toolkit for twenty-first-century preaching. The biggest step in using images is to trust yourself and to have fun embracing the task. This step gets you into the process and opens you to the astonishing possibilities for your sermon. Using images helps your listeners "see" your sermon in a new way and can help make the connection to their personal experiences more profound. Enjoy the journey with images and your listeners will as well. Being boring with powerful images is harder to do. So take on the task and embrace it as a way forward into dynamic and evocative twenty-first-century preaching.

Things to Try on Your Own

1. Keep colored paper and crayons in your desk to play with when you are working on your sermon. Take one verse of one passage and find something that intrigues you enough to draw it. Think about how that one drawing could be related to the congregation and their experiences.

2. Using Play-Doh, create something that comes to your mind after reading several translations of the text for your sermon. Some might even take photographs, to use as bulletin covers if you like what you have created.

3. Create a playful atmosphere in your sermon study group as you prepare weekly for preaching. Play some

music or read poetry together. Create body movements to describe the action in the text or drawings on paper to spark further conversations.

4. Once you have a word, phrase, or image in your mind, go online and do a Google image search. See what images come up related to those words or phrases. These can be a spark for your own creativity. The images can serve as bulletin covers or as part of a media creation for your sermon.

5. Create a PowerPoint, iMovie, or Windows Live Movie Maker video using images you have found. You can use this as an introduction to the sermon or you can have images on the screen slowly moving throughout the sermon. Make sure you use Creative Content images that grant you the right to use them.

6. Plan your images for an upcoming month, season, or quarter. Decide on images for Lent, Easter, or Advent. Utilizing images may drive your worship and preaching planning into new and interesting places. Maybe you can find images of characters at the manger or people at the foot of the cross for a special service. Select images for a service coming up that has deep meaning to your congregation—like Memorial Day or a Christmas Eve Children's Service.

FOUR

To Tweet or Not to Tweet:
Social Media and Preaching

One of the most important processes of preaching is moving with the times, keeping up with the needs of the ever changing world around us. Preachers must be aware that what they do from the pulpit changes with the flow of time and with changes in cultural realities within their context. Preaching has evolved over the centuries, and it is unlikely that that will change as we move forward. It is essential that preachers continue to preach the Good News of Jesus Christ, the power of the cross, the grace of God, and the abundance of the Creator's love for all that exists in the midst of these changes. The message does not change intrinsically; however the method and mode of transmission has changed in the past and will continue to evolve into the future.

In the biblical accounts of Jesus' preaching he passionately told stories that matched the context and the experiences of those to whom he spoke. He spoke to fishermen in analogies that they understood (Matthew 4:18–22 and Luke 5:1–11). For rural, agrarian people he used images of vines, vineyards, and harvests (Luke 10:1–3, Mark 4: 21–34, Luke 13:1–9, and John 15:1–8). He spoke from his heart and brought people into a new understanding of who God meant them to be and how they could experience God's grace and abundant love. He went where the people were. He spent time in their houses of worship and in the homes of friends. He walked the roads with his followers and met people where they were. His words changed people; his touch healed people; his acceptance transformed people; and his life, death, and resurrection changed the world. His words were relevant—before relevant was something cool to be.

There is no evidence that he wrote out anything for his public proclamations, but examples of how and what he taught are provided for us by the Gospel writers. As the church became more established and preachers took on a more significant status, preachers like John Chrysostom spoke extemporaneously on a regular basis. It is even suggested that he would decide on the content of his sermons on the walk to the pulpit from his home. This, however, was possible only because his sermon was conceived after careful and deliberate exegetical study, and he knew his preaching audience for the service. The content of these sermons is available thanks to scribes taking them down word for word as he spoke.

It was after the Reformation and the need for doctrinal consistency in preaching that manuscripts became the norm. Preachers wrote out their sermons carefully to avoid saying something that might rile the political leaders and to avoid becoming too emotional and stating something unintended. This even led some preachers to read their text unemotionally and without any eye contact. These practices spread and continue to affect preaching today. Another reason manuscript preaching spread as a result of the Reformation was that many young preachers were untrained and the new theology of the period was not yet widely understood, so depending on a manuscript was essential.

The move to more impassioned preaching may have begun with Puritan preachers who were committed to preach without notes and who brought to their delivery a high level of emotion. By the end of the eighteen century and at the beginning of the nineteenth the reasons for manuscript preaching were not as prevalent as before, but the practice remained. Passionate preaching began to emerge again, especially in the American frontier denominations.[1] These examples show how preaching has engaged the cultural changes in the past and will continue to evolve with more changes likely on the way.

Passionate and engaging preaching and manuscript preach-ing are not mutually exclusive, but to preach passionately with a manuscript takes intentionality and effort on the part of the preacher. This chapter focuses on one possibility for preaching, which embraces the context of the people and meets them where they are through the use of modes of technology and social media.

Contemporary, technologically driven, and emergent styles of worship are focused on planning, equipping and, embodying themselves for passionate, extemporaneous, contextual, inter-active, and lively preaching that engages the senses in every way possible. Being able to be fluid and flexible on your feet is impera-tive in these settings. However, mainline/main street denomina-tions are also crying out for relevancy, authenticity and connective preaching.[2] Leonard Sweet in *Postmodern Pilgrims* describes the importance of E.P.I.C. elements in worship and preaching as imperative for the twenty-first-century church. He uses this acro-nym to describe worship and preaching for the future. Preaching desperately needs to actively engage persons through *Experience*, *Participation, Images,* and *Connections.* Experiential preaching is interactive and creates an opportunity for the people in the pews to experience God in fresh and profound ways. We are called to help people taste, touch, see, feel, smell, and live the Gospel.

Participatory preaching allows as many people as possible to help plan, lead, and participate in worship. It gets people out of their pews and into a reality often new to them. This type of wor-ship and preaching is invitational. Image-rich preaching honors the visual nature of our culture and of many of our people. Often metaphor and image are more important than words. Connected preaching creates a place and an opportunity for people to belong. It is about helping people feel connected to God, to each other, to the Earth, and even to themselves.[3]

This acronym is helpful for remembering the ways we are called to engage our congregations as we move into the future. To preach in experiential ways means to make real the relationship with God for the people in our pews.[4] We are called to relate the text to the lives of our parishioners, to help make concrete meaning where there might not be any or where there might be confusion. Doing this in ways that allow people to experience God in language, story, and images that are experiential and relevant is important. Doing this in ways that allow people to understand and internalize them is also essential. Providing opportunities for connecting to God in these ways is a vital need of the church today. Lucy Atkinson Rose notes the shift from earlier traditional preaching to new understandings of language, the amazing mystery of all things divine, and the ability of our listeners to tap into their own imaginations.[5] These are important shifts to which the preacher must pay attention. In an age when language and imagination are shifting with the advent of amazing technology for preaching, we are faced with additional issues.

While conversational preaching is not new, it is emerging as an important piece of twenty-first-century proclamation. In preaching there are several ways to be in conversation. One is the manner in which you preach, that is, you preach (speak) in a conversational manner, talking *with* instead of *to* your congregation.[6] This is done by utilizing a more personal tone and speaking style that is more organically conversant. Some talk about this method as speaking in a folksy or natural way from the pulpit or beyond the pulpit area closer to the congregation. This means getting away from a read manuscript or knowing your manuscript so well that you can "speak it" without "reading it." After all, preaching is a spoken event—not a read event—at its core.

Another way to be in conversation is to invite your congregation to respond in the midst of the sermon—to "talk back to you" as you preach. This is common in many traditions, especially in African American churches, but other traditions can also benefit greatly from encouraging congregants to respond in the midst of the sermon. These sermon conversations can be illuminating and exciting. However, you can never plan on what might be shared unless the conversation is more planned than improvisational. The possibilities neverless are exciting. I also suggest that you utilize "plants" in your conversations by inviting several members to be prepared to be one of the early responders. These folks can also speak during lulls in the responses to reengage the sharing if needed.

I mentioned earlier that I have asked folks to call out their favorite foods at church potlucks and got some fun memories stirring in the community. I have also asked for experiences of being lost when I was preaching the three "lost" stories from the Gospel of Luke (Luke 15). One consideration is to make sure you ask for very brief comments and to begin to wrap things up if someone begins to go on too long. Giving up control to allow others to participate can be hard but it can also be empowering for those present who may have never been asked before to share something in the midst of a message.

A third method is to invite conversation before or after the sermon by small group discussion, email, sermon response forms, Facebook discussions, congregational forums, or other media platforms. Social media is an increasingly important part of communication in our world today. In a recent Pew Research Study, which conducted interviews with over two thousand adults who are online at all, 66 percent are on a social media site, such as Facebook, Twitter, MySpace, or LinkedIn.[7] Many of them, according to the research, are connecting on social media sites in order to stay connected with their friends (71 percent of persons 18–29; 70 percent of persons 30–49; 57 percent 50–64; and 45 percent of persons 65+).[8] Over 34 percent of U.S. congregations use both Facebook and a website presence online today. Social media presence is on the rise both for individuals and for churches on a number of levels. Tech is a part of who they are and how they worship: 67 percent of these congregations use major visuals during worship as well. But technology is not the be-all-end-all that some expect.

> Ministry should be, even must be, a technological hybrid venture in this day and age. But technology is not an end in itself. It has to be employed strategically and intentionally as a component of the overall ministry effort of the congregation.[9]

Congregations that employ a high degree of technology grow. And some of them fail. Many are newer congregations with younger members, but not all. Some of them are emergent, some are contemporary, and some are more traditional. Congregations that engage social media and technology run the gamut of congregational types, sizes, and styles. Use of technology and social media can help worship and congregational activities seem more like their own personal everyday experiences. Use of these methodologies can enhance connection between community members and allow for a greater sense of connectedness between leaders and members as well.

It can also show that a ministry is relevant and connected to the contemporary world, especially for members who are younger and already tend to utilize tech and social media in their work, family, and personal lives.[10] What about older members or members not as fluent in social media? The truth is that they are also more connected than you might expect. Many of them had three channels when they got their first TV. In conversations with one of my STM sudents, Blake Scalet, I was reminded once again that they now have access to hundreds of channels from all over the world. They can watch American news shows or the BBC. They can watch House Hunters International to see how folks across the globe evaluate housing options. They can go online and hear music from Argentina or Brazil or Russia. Even adults who are not engaged in frequent social media sites are more globally and technologically connected than ever before. Most have a cell phone and more and more are using smart phones as their primary means of mobile technology. My mother has a Kindle Fire and keeps up with family on Facebook and email, but would not call herself a skilled social media user.

As a preacher, utilizing Facebook or social media groups (or even email groups if that is what your context uses to communicate)—whether lay or clergy—can be a fantastic opportunity to gage the relevancy, engagement, and understanding of your sermons. Using "crowd sourcing"[11] to gain insights from others in the preparation for preaching can be a remarkably insightful way to engage our community. A pastor friend of mine posts on his Facebook status every Monday afternoon the topic or text he is to address the next Sunday in worship. Sometimes he asks for examples of experiences from his "friends," and at other times he asks for initial reactions to the topic or text as he begins to create his sermon. Asking about experiences of doubt on a Facebook status (and also providing for people to respond privately) can give you a sense of where your congregation is as your sermon takes shape.

Providing a Twitter hashtag[12] (like #sermonfeedback_fumc) or other church initials at the end) allows folks to engage you through technological mediums that are comfortable for them after they return home and have digested what was said during the message. Asking members to answer questions after the sermon in these venues will give you a sense of what they heard and how the sermon was received by your members. These social media conversations can be profound and powerful, but they can also serve to disconnect those members who do not use social media at all. Efforts have to be made to be as inclusive of others as possible.

A newer method of conversational preaching proposed by congregations and pastors engaged in the use of technology in church is to engage in electronic "talk back," using Twitter and texting during the sermon itself. Preachers have used this method in various ways, but it is still a fairly uncommon occurrence in most congregations. I find it a wonderful way to engage a group of people for whom social media is the primary means of communicating their thoughts and feelings—maybe even faith—to others. There are a number of ways to utilize this type of crowd sourcing. Some preachers have used this electronic messaging technology by asking their congregation to get out their mobile devices and to send text or Twitter messages of God's love to friends and family during a special Easter service. Or you could have folks send text or Twitter messages about an upcoming sermon series or other messages about your faith community.[13] Some have allowed members to ask them questions about the sermon during its delivery and have answered these questions as they preach. Others have retained these messages and then answered them after the service by the same media, or they have used them to shape a follow-up message for the next sermon.

My own experience with this came about in an intriguing manner. Several years ago I preached at a Youth Rally and on a whim decided to offer those present the chance to text or Tweet me during the sermon. I was preaching about grace and asked for examples of grace in their lives. I got some remarkable texts about parents' acceptance of GLBT children, of teachers' forgiveness of bad behavior, connections to the love of God, and siblings' understanding of bad choices. The stories were remarkably honest and deeply perceptive about what grace meant. I offered the opportunity for them to place a "PVM" at the beginning of the message to denote that they were sending a "private message" not intended to be shared with the wider audience. This gave everyone the chance to share even if their story was not for public discourse.

Others sent stories that were open and to be shared, and as I preached I recounted a few of these. It was a project I had wanted to try for some time, and as I engaged in the practice I found it quite interesting to read the incoming feed while preaching (I use no notes in preaching so I was free to look at these incoming items), but it made for a wild moment or two of intense concentration on trying to determine what I might add from the social media feeds. Some would find this practice too intimidating or too difficult to do simultaneously. For them, other options include crowd sourcing the sermon ahead of time to gather stories or insights that might be added to the sermon for the actual preaching moment. They might also collect the texts and Tweets to be addressed after the sermon or after the service itself in an informal sharing.

Let's look at one biblical text for some inspiration:

> When he returned to Capernaum after some days, it was reported that he was at home. So many gathered around that there was no longer room for them, not even in front of the door; and he was speaking the word to them. Then some people came, bringing to him a paralyzed man, carried by four of them. And when they could not bring him to Jesus because of the crowd, they removed the roof above him; and after having dug through it, they let down the mat on which the paralytic lay. When Jesus saw their faith, he said to the paralytic, "Son, your sins are forgiven." Now some of the scribes were sitting there, questioning in their hearts "Why does this fellow speak in this way? It is blasphemy! Who can forgive sins but God alone?" At once Jesus perceived in his spirit that they were discussing these questions among themselves; and he said to them, "Why do you raise such questions in your hearts? Which is easier, to say to the paralytic, 'Your sins are forgiven,' or to say, 'Stand up and take your mat and walk' "? But so that you may know that the Son of Man has authority on earth to forgive sins'—he said to the paralytic—"I say to you, stand up, take your mat and go to your home." And he stood up, and immediately took the mat and went out before all of them; so that they were

all amazed and glorified God, saying, "We have never seen anything like this!"[14]

There are a number of ways we can engage this text. For me, the most powerful and profound image in the text is of the four persons, likely men, raising the paralyzed man's mat to the roof, breaking through the roofing material, and lowering him right in front of Jesus and the gathered crowd. What an astonishing sight it must have been as the broken roof began to move and light began to seep in through the hole. As it got larger and larger as they dug, what did the people sitting there think was happening? Was the noise level in the room so high that they did not hear the roof being taken apart? Did they cry out in shock or amazement when the man was lowered in front of them? These are important questions for the text. So how might we engage this text through social media? One example is to crowd source ideas about times when you would literally tear through a roof to get to someone. You could ask your Facebook friends the following question for crowd sourcing, "Who would you tear through a roof to get to see or hear?"

You might get answers like Bruce Springsteen or Justin Bieber, or you might get some different and extraordinary answers. You could even couch the question in this way, "If you were ill and heard that Jesus was in your town and speaking at a place down the road from you, what would you do to get to hear him or to be near him?" Or you could start a Twitter hashtag for your congregation about the nature of faith, asking how far your community members would go to help a stranger or friend in a time of need. Your hashtag could be #loweringthemat or #breakingthrutheroof or something else you find inspiring. You can use a number of platforms to crowd source examples of times they went beyond the norm to make something happen for a loved one in need, or you can simply ask for their reactions to the faith of those who lowered the mat, which was enough to move Jesus to heal the paralytic man. It is a powerful story and begs for conversation both before and after the sermon is preached in the community worship service.

To make these activities possible, many technology minded preachers and churches are increasing bandwidth and placing screens in their sanctuaries so that they can accommodate members who ask to Tweet or BBM (BlackBerry Message) or to post chat messages or text messages using their iPhones, Androids, smartphones, or iPads straight onto overhead screens for all to see the interactions between God, the congregants, the message, and the messenger.[15] This kind of electronic engagement allows for immediate reactions and interactions that can be quite profound and personal.

However, there are concerns. "If worship is about creating community, Twitter is an undeniably useful tool. The trick is to not let the chatter overshadow the need for quiet reflection that spirituality requires."[16] Some have called the new age of technology-enmeshed reality a "pseudo reality" or false sense of community. But it is a reality for many. It may be a virtual reality, but for an increasing number of persons the virtual world is how they understand "trans-communication." This communication occurs when individuals are in one physical reality but through technology can also—and at the same time—be conversing and interacting with persons in distant places.[17] This type of interaction to some is isolating and abnormal, but to increasing numbers of Millennials, GenXers, Tweeners, and even older tech-savvy persons this is how they relate—on multiple planes at once. I can be sitting in my comfortable chair in my living room in Philadelphia, chatting on Facebook with my sister in Arlington, Texas, while watching a video of my friend's new home in Seattle, Washington, and receiving a call from my colleague in North Carolina. It is a new era for trans-communication and the church is not immune.

Dwight J. Friesen, in his book *Thy Kingdom Connected*, says that many in today's society, regardless of generational identity, are networked. They are connected to God, to self, and to their community. Often that connection is seen first in the interpersonal connections we have with one person or with groups of persons in physical, social, and conversational interactions. With the advent of social media platforms and networked technology, people are able, like never before, to exist and thrive in multiple states of connection—not just in-person connections, but connections across miles, oceans, cultural differences. We are now able to have amazing connections that are both informal and formal at the same time. We are able to have deep, rich connections with persons we might not ever come in contact with in the non-virtual world.[18] Being willing and able to engage in new networked connections can lead preachers, preaching, and the church into some exciting new possibilities.

An additional concern regarding technology in preaching is the limited number of keyboard characters one can send at any time: 140 for Twitter and 160 for most texting services. How does one ponder deep spiritual or personal questions with others in such short bursts of characters? My own experience has been that most people find ways to communicate with a limited number of characters in creative and powerful ways. Some will find it constrictive, but most will create a way to share their stories. Additionally, with many using abbreviated language or techno-slang on these devices, others in the community who do not participate in these mediums may not even understand the questions being displayed in front of them if they are viewed on a screen in the worship space. These elements of technological interactions with preaching may still be a stretch for many, but I believe that the younger generation's savvy must be engaged.

Preachers may determine that their context is not appropriate for this practice, but the exploration and examination of the issue is important. For increasing numbers of persons, the utilization of these methods of communication will spark great interest. Isn't it worth the conversation—especially if you have persons in your church or community of faith who are already communicating using these methods? It can also lead you to further practices of Web and social media worship. I preached last summer at a church in Brooklyn, New York, called Revolution NYC. There were about forty persons in the room but they webcast the sermon, and during the next week, some six thousand persons heard the sermon and over a hundred interacted with me though email, Twitter, and in the comment section of the webcast. It was an extraordinary experience. And it expanded my understanding of my preaching "audience" in fascinating ways.

Many persons, and possibly even entire congregations, will dismiss this new technology as a passing fad or even as sacrilegious activity in worship. That same complaint, however, is seen throughout history, regarding, for example, organs, church bulletins, guitars, overhead screens, and projectors, to name a few. Even though some will see these developments as distractions or as a secular abomination, they provide persons used to these modes of communication with new and exciting ways to interact with the preacher. Lucy Rose, a proponent of conversational preaching, has advocated inclusion of the congregation in the preaching in intentional ways.[19] To do this utilizing the new technology, we must think outside the traditional ways of gathering a group for conversation before or after the preaching has occurred.

Experiential worship and preaching are important for engaging twenty-first-century congregations, but experiential preaching also can reengage people who have become disillusioned with the church and with worship that seems irrelevant and disconnected in significant ways. Addressing the needs of both the postmodern church and postmodern persons means understanding the shifting ground on which the church exists today.

According to Dan Kimball there are significant shifts in values in the approach to worship and preaching in the modern church, which primarily uses traditional, blended, or contemporary worship styles; the church growth movement, which uses seeker-sensitive worship and preaching to attract new generations; and the emerging church, which is post-seeker-sensitive and follows a different path, a postmodern sensibility, to bring people into the presence of God and to explore their relationship with God through music, images, preaching, technology, and mission.[20] We can learn much from these shifting perspectives.

Preaching has to change to some degree to address the needs of postmoderns and younger generations if we are to embrace a future for the church that includes these generations. Denomination after denomination is in decline. While no one contributing factor can fully explain the losses, one strand of complaint remains in the minds of younger Christians to explain why they are not engaged in religious communities: they find the worship and preaching to be boring, irrelevant, and unrelatable to their lives.[21]

Leonard Sweet describes the world as being divided into two dominant groups: "Gutenbergers" and "Googlers."[22] Gutenbergers are people of the book. They love to hold a book in their hands and read printed text off a page. They long for the scent of an old book. They learn about and engage the world through print. They still read newspapers and like their world to be uncluttered by technology and the concerns of that lifestyle. My parents and many of their generation belong to this group. They get their news from nightly news broadcasts and the daily paper delivered to their doorstep. My mother does use email to communicate and has a Facebook account, but her level of expertise and knowledge of the site are not the best. The principal form of communication for Gutenbergers is the phone, and they still have a landline.

Googlers, on the other hand, are drenched with the world of technology. They carry around their lives—calendars, the Internet, contacts, calling plans, GPS capabilities, and games—on their smart phones and iPads. They engage their friends through Facebook, Twitter, texting, and other social media platforms. They are more apt to find their news on Google Reader, HuffPo,[23] or a favorite blog than on TV or a mainstream news outlet. This is my generation. We would be lost without our "tethers," our phones. We don't have a landline. We use social media with ease but did not grow up with it. We adjusted easily as it emerged on the scene. My fourteen-year-old son is a tech-immersed child of social media. He uses his phone to text and talks to his friends by Oovoo or Skype (video calling platforms). He has his own YouTube channel and never "learned" to use the new technology; he simply grew up in that milieu. According to Sweet, above all else Googlers have adapted the available technologies of the modern age allowing them to engage the "core human longings: knowing, being known, belonging, perception."[24]

The question becomes, How do we address the requirements of preaching the Gospel of Jesus Christ, affirm the needs of techno-savvy congregants, and not bring on a free-for-all in the pulpit? And can we do this for both Gutenbergers and Googlers? We need guidelines to help preachers understand what elements of modern technology to bring into their preaching moment, if they choose to do so.

First, as always preachers must know their context and the people in their congregation. Smart preachers will remember the extremely important adage—"context, context, context." Remember and honor your context. When I was in seminary, my ethics professor, Dr. Emilie Townes, taught us that getting to know the people with whom we will work and to whom we will preach the Gospel means we must pitch our tent with them as pilgrims instead of tourists. Tourists visit a place but stay aloof from the goings-on in the place. They buy souvenirs, take photos, eat food familiar to them, and keep their own customs and traditions for the most part. In contrast, pilgrims come to pitch their tent with the natives. They learn the language and come to appreciate and live into the customs, foods, traditions, and dress of the people with whom they have come to live. Their behavior changes, their understanding of the world changes, and their ways of communicating change. Pilgrims preach in ways that are relevant and connected to the natives. Tourists preach as if they are staying for only a brief time and are not fully committed to getting to know the people and serve as a part of the community, living fully among them.[25] To be the preacher for your community of faith means taking this contextual responsibility to its fullest possible extent.

The pulpit is an important place to be, and preachers who do not take the pulpit seriously and do not get to know the persons to whom they are speaking are apt to make some serious mistakes in trying to connect the message with the people. Knowing, for example, where they work, what they do for entertainment, where their kids go to school, how they might be related to each other, etc., is important. Context is key. This is true for all aspects of preaching but in engaging technology, it is essential. Preachers need to determine whether their congregation includes significant numbers of persons, Googlers or techno-savvy folks, for whom the technology would be a welcome addition. One could do a survey of the congregation or simply experiment with initial Tweeting or texting in church or Facebook dialogues to gauge the level of interest. The preacher should be cautious and courteous in these attempts and in making these decisions.

Second, if there are significant numbers of persons interested, the preacher must then determine if there are also some in the community both Gutenbergers and others who would find the technology distracting or unhelpful. These people's wishes must also be acknowledged. This does not mean that a preacher would decide not to engage technology in preaching, but it does mean that the ways to use the technology may need to be determined more judiciously. Some congregations have chosen to bring technology only into more emergent or contemporary services while keeping it out of the more traditional ones. Some have used it sparingly for specific holiday sermons or for a particular sermon or series. Others have made use of small-group technology-based discussions to augment their worship services as a trial run. There are many options a church can experiment with. There is an intriguing idea in the "Things to Try on Your Own . . . " section of this chapter. It describes a first attempt at texting with a designated person from your congregation serving as a moderator during a worship service to receive and respond to texts.

Third, preachers must assess the space in which they preach to evaluate the possibilities. Tweeting, texting, and Facebook status updates during worship are essential. Upgrades can be added by installing wireless routers in the sanctuary or worship area. To have texts or Tweets displayed on an overhead screen requires appropriate equipment (more about this in chapter 5). Lower tech churches can ask members to participate in technological practices when they are home as well, but the efficacy is likely to decline once members leave the worship space. Adding technological capabilities is becoming less and less costly.

Fourth and most important, preachers must determine if the use of technology is in line with the message they are preaching and in tune with the Gospel of Jesus Christ. I have attended worship services where the technology was more rock concert than worship. And for those present the reactions were mixed. I saw people thoroughly engaged with the imagery and lights with eyes wide to take it all in. I also saw people cringing from the onslaught of visual stimulus. I attended one service with my parents and my nieces; I saw both ends of the age spectrum sitting right next to me. My dad was visibly uncomfortable and was covering his ears at times. My nieces were watching with awe and were moving with the music.

At times it was even a bit too much for me, and I am a Googler. But I have seen technology as a contributing factor enabling people to connect to the message. One instance was in an emergent worship service in downtown Philadelphia. The pastor was preaching a sermon on sharing one's faith with others on a personal and more consistent basis. Several persons there, myself included, got ready for the typical evangelism sermon. However, that is not what happened.

Instead, the pastor showed a video clip of a recent mission trip the congregation had made, and we learned that he had previously asked for persons who had posted on social media sites to send links to him. What popped up next on the screen were Tweets, Facebook status updates, Flickr photos, personal blog posts, and YouTube videos from the trip. The remarkable thing was seeing the responses to these pictures, short bursts of information sharing, and video clips. There were about forty different social media examples shared with the congregation with over four hundred responses, retweets, and blog comments. There had been eighteen people on the trip, but thousands were made aware of the mission of the church and how they shared the love of Jesus with those the members encountered.

The pastor made use of the social media attention by inviting those who responded to participate in a local short-term mission project to get them engaged in living their faith missionally. More than fifty people showed up—many with no connection to the congregation except for the social media exchanges about the trip. This pastor's use of technology was completely in line with the technologically savvy persons in their church and with the message he was presenting about living one's faith and sharing that with others. It was an extraordinary sight. Yes, it might have happened using other media, but the immediacy of the responses and the quick planning of a way to capture the excitement meant a group of persons were engaged by a message of faithful discipleship using a medium that folks were personally connected to already.

Adam Thomas reminds us that time itself is important to everyone. Some feel like we never have enough of it, and some feel as if they need every advantage in this fast-paced world. Spending time in worship is a choice, and we must value the time persons have put into being present with God and our communities of faith. Technology can make the time even more valuable to some while others will see it as an intrusion into their quiet time with God. Time that people spend as part of a faith community is time they have committed to connection, covenant, and community. We have to honor that. Worship and preaching in the digital age are like Christ's time: it is not something we can define or limit. It is like baseball time: it takes as long as it takes.[26] Using trans-communication—communicating on a number of personal and technological levels—is one way to make real-time connections to those present in powerful and profound ways. And in a changing time like this, preaching in new and techno-savvy ways for some makes the time spent even more relevant and engaging.

Experiential worship, E.P.I.C. worship/preaching, and embracing technology in preaching engages the entire person: heart, soul, mind, and strength—which is our call in preaching and worship. The act of creating connection in preaching means we refuse to preach boring sermons, and we will create opportunities for our communities of faith to experience an encounter with God that is profound and personal and at the same time communal and connective.[27] True worship is about more than singing songs, reading texts, or arguing about worship styles; it is about something much deeper.[28]

As Kim Miller says in *Designing Worship: Creating and Integrating Powerful God Experiences*, churches embracing the needs of postmoderns and techno-savvy persons are not concerned with the ninety-nine sheep safely in the fold (traditional churches or congregations meeting their needs). They are more concerned with the one lost sheep in need of rescue. Creating a worship experience and a preaching moment for the postmodern ethos means embracing "the challenge of dreaming up new ways to search for sheep in a postmodern [and technology savvy] culture, . . . to create wonderful and imaginative worship experiences that will entice the one lost sheep back into the fold."[29] To preach in this ethos and connect to new generations, these issues must be kept in mind. Utilizing technology to connect to the one lost sheep is one way to do just that. And engaging in these technological practices may even reinvigorate some of the ninety-nine already there. Preaching into and in the future cannot afford to ignore these needs. Preaching that utilizes social media is many things, but usually it is not boring.

Things to Try on Your Own

1. A first step is to try to use social media in a controlled setting. If you have a Facebook or other social media page, try asking for insights about an upcoming sermon topic or text. Ask a very direct question like, "When you read the story of the Samaritan Woman (John 4) what parts of the story speak to you?" or "Has there been a time when you received unconditional grace in your life? What did that feel like?" Use the responses either in your sermon preparation or in a section of your sermon where it seems appropriate. Offer folks the chance to reply either publicly (on your post or through a direct inbox or email message).

2. Crowd source a sermon's image by asking for a favorite picture that shows the power of love. Examine the images sent or suggested to see which would be appropriate for the sermon and the context of your congrega-

tion. Use an image in your worship media or as a bulletin cover. You can also crowd source a movie or video that folks find particularly important in their understanding of love.

3. Try social media in a worship service by simply asking all present to get out their phones and send out a message of love and acceptance. Ask them to text or email one person who they think might need to hear a word of love and acceptance in their lives. You can do this on a special Sunday, like Easter or Christmas, when you may also have a packed house or on some other important time in the life of your community of faith. Have them text or email about Fall Kick-off Sunday or an upcoming worship series. Or have them contact legislators or political leaders to advocate for a social issue important to the community.

4. Utilize social media in your worship service. Ask someone from your worship committee or someone on staff who has a depth of knowledge about the liturgy to be the point person for a Texting Sunday. Print the phone number in the bulletin and post it on the screen if you are using visual technology in your service. Invite persons to ask questions of the point person about what is happening in worship, why we do the things we do, or how they might better participate or understand the actions in the service. That person can then respond individually and directly to those questions. I have served in this capacity and have gotten some interesting questions. I was asked why we dip communion bread into the cup rather than eating it separately and drinking from the cup, what our Pastoral Fund Offering went to support, and why giving up our fears is so hard, among others.

I found the exercise invigorating. I had over fifty questions and responses during that worship service. But everyone had their phones on silent or vibrate and no one seemed to be bothered by the activity. The breadth and depth of questions asked in 140 characters or less was amazing. Each time we have done this, increasing numbers of folks have participated in the texting.

5. Try something bolder and allow questions and comments during the sermon. Have a moderator screen the questions before posting onto a screen for all to see. Or you can hold on to them until after the sermon so that you can spend some time answering the questions with the congregation. To be even more boldly engaged with social media, as the posts come up, you can comment or add the items into the sermon or simply have them posted for others to read.

FIVE

Screens in Worship:
"Over My Dead Body!" or "Let's Do It!"

(A brief chapter on buying and using technology gear resources)

Many churches today are debating whether to include visual technology options in their worship spaces. Some are adding screens and projectors with little regard for how or why. Some are having serious theological discussions about what technology can do in worship and what it can't. These groups are creating plans for the use of technology in their worship services that are cogent and constructive. Some have decided, however, that adding screens and projectors is not appropriate for their context and community at this time and maybe forever, but they are at least attending to the question. Some are creating plans to engage technology but have little in the way of resources to make these plans a reality. So what do we say about screens in worship? Recently on his Facebook status Leonard Sweet posted the following update about technology, worship, and liturgical space: "What if we approached sanctuaries as smart rooms: You're all preachers. How do we capture the wisdom/messages in this room?"[1] What a profound question, and it is one that I have dealt with often.

When I first encountered the debate, I was pastoring a church in northern New Jersey that shared space with a Korean congregation. The Korean congregation was engaged in more contemporary worship than my community was at the time, and they wanted to install a screen and projector to utilize in worship. They wanted to put lyrics of songs on the screen, show video clips, and put up the preacher's sermon outline for folks, whether first-generation Korean speakers or second- and third-generation English speakers, to keep up with the service, which was often celebrated in a bilingual manner. They approached the chair of our building committee and me about having a conversation to approve such a purchase and installation. During one of the first meetings, I heard one of my members say the dreaded words about technology in worship: "Over my dead body will you put screens in that sanctuary." Instead of letting that be the last word, we engaged in thoughtful conversation about his concerns, created space to hear positives and negatives about installation and possible uses for the media, and eventually went to visit several area churches that had recently installed similar technology. It took a while, but we got to the point that everyone, even the "over my dead body" opponent, was ready to commit. That took patience, listening to concerns, honoring where people were on the issue, pointing out new possibilities, and really discussing honestly and openly who we wanted to be as a relevant community of faith in the twenty-first century.

One of the concerns was to preserve the aesthetics of the sanctuary. We did some intense research and found a remote controlled screen that could be housed in a box overhead that was concealed behind a ceiling beam. From the back, if the screen was not down, you could not see the screen at all. And the projector was on a metal rod housed in a box painted the same color as the ceiling. If you were in front of the sanctuary looking to the back of the room you could see it, but other than that it was pretty well obscured. We had addressed the aesthetic issues and all involved seemed pleased with the results. The building was very old and we took care to keep the integrity of the space and all that had and would take place in the room.

The next step was to determine a plan of use for our new technology. The majority of my congregation did not want to "lose" our more traditional mode of worship, but we now had access to visual technology in our space and needed to determine if and when we might avail ourselves of its possibilities. So we went through a series of discussions about the pluses and minuses of tech use. We recognized that we still enjoyed hymn singing and did not have a strong music leadership team that could pull off a new, music-oriented use of the screens. So we decided that no change was necessary, and everyone basically got on board with this.

Next we discussed whether we wanted to utilize the tech gear for announcements prior to worship and to show United Methodist resource videos or Conference and District promotional videos for upcoming events or for missional education. The decision was fairly easy to make since almost all who were part of the Visual Technology Team and many in the congregation were frustrated with either starting the service with a list of read announcements or with breaking the "flow" of the service later on to make these announcements. Our Visual Technology Team was made up of myself and three congregation members: one person was our tech guru since her professional life and hobby were in IT; one person was very interested in finding photos and videos and served as our back-up IT person; and the third person was our organist/musician who wanted to be part of the discussion to enhance our congregational music life through tech whenever possible.

So our first use of the screen and projector was to display announceents and advertisements prior to worship. This practice was met with a great response. Folks loved the visual images displayed with the announcements and found that they remembered them better when we made short videos to announce coming events. A funny thirty-second clip about our upcoming

Garrumage Sale (a combo of garage and rummage sales) brought out more donations than ever before. And people then clamored to be part of adverts for upcoming events. It was great fun to be a part of that process. We used a Flip camera to record the clips and uploaded them to the laptop used for worship to show them as part of our opening announcement time. We discovered that we had untapped talents in our church that we never knew about. Folks who had acted in prior periods in their lives came out of the woodwork to volunteer. And the inherent humor and fun of our community came out in the videos they created. A new air of engagement stirred among us. Folks who did not know each other well became friends through this work. It became one of the most inter-generational ministries of our church.

The next decision concerned how to utilize the visual technology in preaching. I am a no notes preacher, so putting up an outline made me nervous since I was known to move things into a different order as I preached. I think my own discomfort meant this was not a way we would utilize the tech. I was aware that there are a variety of other vital ways which visual technology could be beneficial to my preaching. However, I also knew that a few people in the church were still nervous about using tech in worship. We had made progress with the advert videos, but I did not want to overwhelm those who still needed some level of caution. Even though we had a unanimous vote to go ahead with the purchase and installation, Dead Body Bob was still worried that the media would overshadow the message. We waited for an opportunity and for a good reason to arise so that we could incorporate the use of visual media into the church service itself.

We spent months thinking, talking, and planning. As a team, we decided adding video or still images to preaching called for careful steps. The congregation had accepted the announcements, but we did not want to go overboard with our first use of the visual technology in the preaching moment in ways that might alienate some of the more cautious or concerned members. We had to determine if we would use still photos or moving images. The decision was one we spent a lot of time contemplating. I had spent some time alone thinking about my role as pastor, about my own biased wishes, and about the decision as it related to the critical needs of the congregation. We also spent considerable time discussing it as the Visual Technology Team for our congregation.

We knew that our congregation includes many former military personnel and many who were parents of active duty personnel as part of a typical Sunday's gathered community. About a month before Memorial Day, we asked if people would be willing to share photos of persons serving in the military, past or present, to be brought in or emailed to the office. We invited all current and past members of the church and their extended families to participate. Dozens of photos were shared. We had pictures from just about every military conflict in the modern era and from virtually every branch of the armed forces. From this offering of images I created a Windows Media Movie, with background music, highlighting the images of the shared photos. People wept and laughed at the diversity of images and memories that flooded the sanctuary.

Some were poignant, and moving, some were funny, and some were just head shots of loved ones taken during a leave with or without their family. Never again did anyone complain about the use of the projector or the screen. I did not force the use on the members, nor did I use canned videos that might not register with my context. I utilized the technology for a Sunday that was significant for them and made their images come to life before their eyes. It was a moving tribute that was shared during the introduction to our prayer time and then names were read aloud during the prayer itself. The combination of technology and personal memories was profound and powerful. "Bob" approached me after the service, with tears in his eyes, saying, "If you can make moments like that in worship, I won't stand in your way ever again. Thanks for that." It was a big moment for our church and for my understanding of the power of images (still and moving) and tech gear to transform the possibilities for engagement in worship on many levels.

You can record advertisements, document testimonials or personal stories, promote upcoming mission trips, show interviews of members, display videos related to preaching—these and many other uses can have great effect. Knowing what you want to do is essential. Then take the time to make critical decisions about whether the use is appropriate for your community. Your team has to make the essential decisions to critique the images and videos for inclusivity, appropriate language, relevancy to the message and context, and theology consistent with the community.

The next important task for the preacher and team as they utilize imagery is to take these same critical skills and turn them to the use of moving images. Many companies sell videos for use in worship. Many are sold as packages that correlate with a themed sermon series or are related to texts (either series based or lectionary based). Some of these are quite powerful and useful. Some are actually offensive in their language and lack of inclusivity. But you should visit:

- www.GodTube.com
- www.worshiphousemedia.com
- www.vimeo.com
- www.motionworship.com
- www.sermonspice.com

See what else is available and then critically analyze the resources for use in your context. You can also create videos for use in your own congregation.

An initial point is that you have to have a laptop computer capable of doing media production, editing, running DVDs, connecting to projectors, and media sharing. Many pastors have their own laptops for personal use, and these can be used for media technology purchases. That means, however, that when the pastor leaves, the computer may leave as well, leaving the church without a computer to run its system. Acquiring a laptop that is powerful and portable is a first step in this journey toward utilizing technology in worship. Once this is completed, you can begin the next steps. Purchasing projectors and screens can be quite costly. Depending on the space and the media needs of the congregation, projectors can be found that will be more than adequate and that will be cost-effective. Some congregations that worship in smaller spaces have opted for 60 to 90 inch HD TVs instead of a projector and screen.

For them, this is a logical and effective choice; however it does not provide adequate viewing options in larger spaces, which require enormous screens that cost hundreds of thousands of dollars. Doing your research is important. The lighting of the sanctuary or worship space will determine whether the projector system needs to be front- or rear-projecting.[2] Getting a projector that has the appropriate brightness to deal with the ambient light in the space is pivotal to the overall successful inclusion of a projector. Many companies will come to your location and do a light and projector analysis to help you in this process. Being prepared to do the work to determine what system best fits your space is essential. Utilizing an independent technology consultant or a system company that provides spatial consulting can save you time and energy in doing the necessary research into your congregational and technological needs. There are, however, other options that are less expensive. Some churches could consider using a blank wall that is unobstructed to make use of technology more economical—even though it might not provide optimum viewing.

A rolling cart for your projection system so that it is more mobile, instead of a ceiling-mounted system, can also decrease costs and allow for multiple space usage for the projector as well. Churches need to do research, calculate their available and potential funds, and create a strategy that allows for staged implementation of their technology plan. Each church needs to make decisions that make sense for their circumstances. Using a team for the planning and research allows for a diversity of expertise and opinions in the process. This team idea is necessary as you move forward. Your team can plan for weekly usage of your technology. They need to practice ahead of time so that the timing can be worked out and any glitches can be worked through. One of the keys to remember is that using technology comes with the inherent danger of "tech fails." At one point or another your technology will fail you on the spot.

A computer will fail to load, a bulb will blow when you don't have a replacement, a system will fail to boot up, a slide show will be corrupted or fail to transition slides in the way intended, the wrong screen will be displayed during congregational singing. Surviving these moments, with patience and persistence, is important. This highlights the need to practice and to plan the use of any tech gear for any given worship experience.[3]

With all the Web-based resources and computer programs that help with text-based images, still images, and moving image video production, just about anyone can get into the act of designing for worship and preaching. Simple announcements require little more than a PowerPoint or Keynote presentation program. Little cost, above the initial output of money for a screen and projector, is required. Many churches cannot begin to budget for a staff member for visual technology, but most have someone in their community of faith who deals with these programs in their daily work lives and who might be willing to take on the task or to train others for this kind of ministry. Most teenagers use these programs in school, and if you have a responsible teen in your community of faith who is able and interested, you might ask him or her to serve in this capacity or train several adults to do this work. Asking these persons to share their expertise can be the first step in creating a new Visual Technology Team for your church. Additionally, many of these programs come preloaded on your computer or laptop.

One of the most powerful developments in my congregation and, in my experience, that of many others was that the screens helped us to move into a more relevant and vital worship style. And it was more indigenous to the current context of the world. Many of my congregants were no longer "people of the book"; they had already begun to be "people of the screen." This new worship, while not totally different, started attracting younger members and families with kids. It was a vital and vibrant time for the church, and I believe our changes in worship and the use of visual technology helped move us forward.

We must, however, address the issue of the rapid pace of changing technology in our culture. The speed with which technological changes is occurring is mind-boggling. Every day there seem to be new social media platforms introduced, new types of sharing devices, and enhancements to already existing technology. Projectors from the early 2000s are already out of date with the changing technology and increased screen resolution. A church trying to "keep up" with all these changes may find it a fruitless endeavor. Within months of the introduction of the Apple iPad, applications for preaching and even the iPulpit (or iPodium) had been developed to enhance the use of the iPad and other tablet devices in preaching.[4] The iPulpit is a pulpit with a docking station for an iPad. It allows users to easily dock their iPad or other tablet device for use in preaching, for utilizing social media, and for running visual technology equipment. While some will find this a ridiculous item, other "geeked-out" pastors and churches will disregard the $800 price tag and buy one for their church. I might be one of the first to sign up for such an item. But many communities of faith have gone to great lengths to secure the funding to purchase visual technology devices and even thinking about upgrading on a regular basis is out of the question. Such is the pace of technology changes in our culture. Churches need to assess where they want to be in the use of technology and how their technology dollars will be spent so that they do not become overwhelmed with all of the options available. We live in an ever changing time.

Taking the time necessary for research, analysis, conversations, experimentation, and practice is the key to successful tech use in the church today. There are a number of excellent media resources listed in the bibliography of this book for your use as well. A few of them even have step-by-step instructions on how to create media for worship. This type of inclusion of tech gear may not work in your context, but the discussions need to happen so that all of the twenty-first-century possibilities of worship are explored for you and your community of faith. Above all else, don't be overwhelmed by the tech. Let it enhance what you do and open doors for new discovery for your worship now and into the future.

Preaching boring sermons with technology is still a possibility, but having the visual images and the connections to them in your worship and preaching lessens the chances. Take the chance and engage these ideas as much as you and your church can.

What's Next for Preaching . . . And for You?

As I stated at the very beginning of this book, I believe there needs to be a change in twenty-first-century preaching. We need to do everything we can to avoid preaching boring sermons. So preaching needs to be more engaging, more image-rich, more narrative, more relational, more creative, more authentic, more conversational, more socially connected, and more imaginative. It may, depending on the community concerns and interests, also need to be more connected to social media and engaged with technological options for worship and beyond. To achieve this, preachers must be committed to the process of change and open to new ideas for their preaching.

Preachers have to take the plunge into the deep end of the pool and be willing to try new things. Most preachers get used to one style of preaching. Maybe that is how they were taught in seminary or divinity school. Maybe it is from years of watching a mentor pastor preach in their home church. Maybe that style comes from watching a favorite TV preacher. But taking the time to wade beyond what is comfortable is important. You might just need to put some floaties on and try things in this book that are less frightening or intimidating to you. You might want to step out in faith and move into deeper water by stretching yourself to go chest-deep in the water by trying things that are a bit more challenging to you. Or you might want to climb right up to the high board and dive right in to some of the most challenging parts of this book. You know yourself better than anyone else. Pay attention to what activities draw you to experiment with them and what makes you nervous or anxious. Those are clues to ways you can engage the activities included in this book. Whatever your decision is about the depth that you are comfortable with, putting on your swimsuit and getting wet is an important first step. Trying the things you are more comfortably drawn to is okay. But you might also want to pay attention to what scares you most and gently move into those areas as well.

Additionally, preachers have to be ready to bring new energy and creative dynamics to their sermons. They have to step out of their academic and theologically deep language and speak to their people in ways that are relational and personal. Preachers have to put more of themselves into the creative process of crafting sermons. This does not mean sharing your personal stories every week; it means putting your imagination and creativity into the initial stages of writing that go beyond exegeting the text. It means speaking truth about the current world circumstances. Karl Barth tells us that preachers should preach with a newspaper in one hand and a Bible in the other. Perhaps the analogy today means preaching with an iPad in one hand and a Bible in the other.

Regardless of where you get your news, you need to be current and relevant in your preaching. You need to know your context so well that your stories, illustrations, and images match who your listeners are. You need to address your context in ways that connect to their lives. You need to let your listeners know you are "with" them. To do this you need to be engaged, relational, and connected. And you need to be willing to be totally immersed in the creative process of play. Playing with the text and the sermon preparation process is a big part of this. Nevertheless, I cannot ever remember being told in seminary to play when I was planning and writing a sermon. You have permission. Go right ahead and play. It may take a while for you to be completely comfortable with this, but it is a task in which we should all be actively engaged.

There needs to be some concrete preparation for the listeners, as well. As preachers, we have a level of power that those sitting in the pews do not. They get to listen and respond, but we decide what is preached and how it is preached. Even if we use a set of lectionary readings that are a part of our church's tradition, the preacher is still likely to decide which text to address more directly in the sermon and in what direction to take the sermon. There are multiple layers of meaning in the biblical texts we preach about on any given Sunday, and the preacher is the one who spends the most time with them, refining the images to use, analyzing the stories to tell, deciding the theological concepts to address, and determining the shape of the sermon. We have to use this power carefully. We may have a worship team or a committee that helps plan our worship time as communities of faith, but the preacher still holds the preponderance of the power. Help your listeners hear your sermons better by engaging them concretely, letting them participate in crowd sourcing, asking them to read the texts you will be preaching about ahead of time, and being as relevant as you can be in your preaching.

We also have to begin the preparation process early enough in the week so that we have time to play, to analyze, to write, to edit, to spend time with images and story, and to let all of this marinate in our hearts and minds. My seminary preaching professor Eugene Lowry taught us to start early in the week so that we can let all of our initial impressions, our research, our readings, and our commentary exegesis marinate for a while. When we cook meat that is marinated, we let it have time to soak in the marinade. If you don't allow the marinade to soak in, there is no effect on the meat. You have to spend time soaking in your sermon "stuff." You have to walk around with your thoughts in your heart and head. You have to play with the images, turn the trajectory of the sermon over and over in your mind to see what works better, and let the material you have found in the culture around you and in your readings guide your thoughts on the text. Marinating takes time. Because of this need for time, sermons that are "Saturday Night Specials" are not optimal, they do not allow time for marinating. Waiting too late in the week, or until Saturday evening, to write a sermon barely gives you time for cooking at all. So making a decision to start earlier in the week can be a simple yet powerful act of giving your preaching the time it needs for marinating. I believe this is a great step in making your preaching more powerful and less likely to be boring.

Just spending more time on it and asking the important questions that need asking as you prepare can make all the difference in the world to your preaching and therefore for your listeners. Occasionally, events happen in the week that leave you in a bind, and Saturday night is the only time you have to work on your sermon, but this should not be your normative practice. Working to set up a new pattern will give you time to work on your preaching at a whole new level of engagement.

In all of this you need to be authentic and true to yourself. When we preach we have to be ourselves. Our listeners will know if we are not being "real" with them. They can see and hear it as we preach. You should not try to be something you aren't, but you can grow and stretch your skills and expectations. You should not mimic someone else's style, but you can try out the patterns and suggestions of others. You also should not sit back knowing you need to grow as a preacher and refuse to make any changes.

If you are preaching boring or less than inspiring sermons week in and week out, if you just have an "off" Sunday from time to time, or if you just want to lessen the possibilities of preaching a boring sermon, these steps on the path to more engaging preaching are important ones. Engaging in new practices, trying new ideas, giving yourself and your sermon time, and engaging your imagination are powerful tools. Making the decision to work on your preaching is a pivotal moment in your ministry. And it rests in your hands, mostly.

Yes, the decision to make changes in preaching is often in the hands of the preacher. Preachers often sense that they need to try new things or are hungering for a new vitality in their preaching. I, too, had that awakening in my own preaching earlier in my career. I have known congregations to address the preacher's shortcomings in the pulpit and suggest (sometimes strongly) that they work on their preaching and make some changes in how or what they preach so that they engage the listeners better than they previously had been. No matter the reason for picking up a book on improving your preaching, you have made the decision to make changes or at the very least to evaluate your own preaching routine within some new possibilities. And that is significant.

Whether you believe your preaching is superb or sub-par, the path to changing your preaching in significant and powerful ways is a choice. I hope and pray that you try some of these activities, methods, and ideas. Utilize the "Things to Try on Your Own" sections at the end of each chapter. The more you put into the process of engaging narrativity, creativity, images, social media, and technology the more you and your community of faith—your listeners—will get out of the efforts. The Gospel of Jesus deserves this effort. The people sitting in our worship experiences deserve this effort. Being true to our calling as preachers of the Word deserves it.

I thank God that you have joined me on this journey of twenty-first-century preaching. I hope it lessens the chance you'll ever again be boring from the pulpit.

Keep on refusing to preach another boring sermon.

Notes

Introduction

1. Leonard I. Sweet introduced me to this phrase about preaching in a conversation at Drew Theological School in Madison, New Jersey, in 2002. He said that preachers too often spend more time perfecting the theology and language of their sermon than determining if the sermon actually "preaches." He was spot on with regard to a lot of preachers.

2. "101 Things to Do during a Dull Sermon." www.christianforums.com/t18165.

3. "Youth Ministry 3.0 Quotes." http://theoquest.blogspot.com/2009_06_01_archive.html.

4. "Why 100% of Young People Dread the Sermon." http://churchnext.tv/2012/08/20/stephen-cady

5. Leonard I. Sweet, "The Quest for Community," *Leadership Journal* 20, no. 4 (Fall 1999): 33.

6. David L. Schlafer. *Surviving the Sermon: A Guide to Preaching for Those Who Have to Listen* (Boston: Cowley Publishing, 1992), 7.

Chapter 1: I Love to Tell the Story

1. Mark Miller, *Experiential Storytelling: (Re)Discovering Narrative to Communicate God's Message* (Grand Rapids: Zondervan Publishing, 2003), 7.

2. Graham Johnston, *Preaching to a Postmodern World: A Guide to Reaching Twenty-First Century Listeners* (Grand Rapids: Baker Books, 2001), 161.

3. John C. Holbert and Alyce M. McKenzie, *What Not to Say: Avoiding the Common Mistakes That Can Sink Your Sermon* (Louisville: Westminster John Knox Press, 2011), 88.

4. Johnston, *Preaching to a Postmodern World*, 93.

5. Ibid., 155.

6. My father, a United Methodist preacher, heard this story for the first time from one of his Old Testament professors at Perkins School of Theology at Southern Methodist University in the late 1950s.

7. Genesis 25:19–34.

8. Johnston, *Preaching to a Postmodern World,* 157.

9. Miller, *Experiential Storytelling* , 41.

10. Genesis 25:19–34.

11. Heather Murray Elkins, "Altar-ing the World: Community-forming Word and Worship," in *Preaching in the Context of Worship*, ed. David M. Greenhaw and Ronald J. Allen (St. Louis: Chalice Press, 2000), 16.

12. This style of preaching emerged in the 1950s and beyond and changed preaching, both in the pulpits of our churches and in the Academy of Homiletics, the academic guild of preaching teachers and professors. It was led by Fred Craddock, Eugene Lowry, and others. Paul Scott Wilson, "New Homiletic" in *New Interpreter's Handbook of Preaching* (Nashville: Abingdon Press, 2008), 398–99.

13. Johnston, *Preaching to a Postmodern World,* 163.

14. Alyce M. McKenzie, *Novel Preaching: Tips from Top Writers on Crafting Creative Sermons* (Louisville: Westminster John Knox Press, 2010), 7.

15. Ibid.

16. Ibid., 49

17. Sondra B. Willobee, *The Write Stuff: Crafting Sermons That Capture and Convince* (Louisville: Westminster John Knox Press, 2009), 29ff.

18. Ibid.

19. Joseph M. Webb, *Preaching without Notes* (Nashville: Abingdon Press, 2001), 25.

20. Ibid.

21. Ibid., 29.

22. Ibid.

23. Ibid., 25–29.

Chapter 2: Preaching and the Hokey-Pokey

1. "Plants" are persons in your congregation whom you have made aware of an upcoming worship activity and have asked them to participate early on to help lessen the anxiety of others. On several occasions I have used plants to augment activities I was planning. This has allowed me to try some new and inventive things and know ahead of time that I would have some degree of "buy in" from, at the very least, those I had asked to help in the activity. What I have learned from experience is that others who see plants participate will follow suit more willingly than if there is no plant present.

2. A copy of the letter was sent to me with the DVD, and I cherish it. I have used a different name and changed some of the particular circumstances.

3. People understand exegesis in a number of ways. Essentially it means doing study and research on a biblical text and its multiple meanings. Traditionally exegesis has included historical and cultural analysis, word studies in the original languages, author studies to determine who wrote the text and to whom, critical interpretation, and discovering the relevancy of the text for the audience to whom it will be taught or preached.

4. Julia Cameron, *The Artist's Way: A Spiritual Path to Higher Creativity* (New York: G. Putnam's Sons, 1992).

5. Ibid., 117–26.

6. Ibid., 194–95.

7. The first time I heard this idea as a preaching exercise was from Thomas H. Troeger at the 2006 Academy of Homiletics Annual Meeting in Florida during the Narrative and Imagination Working Group.

8 Matthew 14:13–21.

9. Alyce M. McKenzie, *Novel Preaching: Tips from Top Writers on Crafting Creative Sermons* (Louisville: Westminster John Knox Press, 2010), 13.

10. Ibid., 11–26.

11. Sondra B. Willobee, *The Write Stuff: Crafting Sermons That Capture and Convince* (Louisville: Westminster John Knox Press, 2009), 11–28.

12. Willobee, *The Write Stuff*, 67–68.

13. With a small journal that you can carry around wherever you go this is easy. However, there are also numerous digital methods as well. You can use your smart phone, iPad, or digital recorder to record your thoughts. Some folks prefer to write out their thoughts while others prefer to speak them. Experiment with what works for you and keep that method available to you as you go through your day. I personally keep a small notebook (2" x 4") in my briefcase and in my travel bag. But I also have access to my phone or iPad if I do not have my briefcase with me. Using a cloud service to keep your notes (like Google docs or Evernote, among others) means you can have access to your thoughts on multiple platforms.

14. Cameron, *The Artist's Way*.

15. This list of biblical passages was developed by my teaching assistant Leah Schade for Next Level Preaching, an advanced elective offered in the 2011 spring semester at the Lutheran Theological Seminary at Philadelphia.

16. Other Web-based photo sites have these search capabilities as well. In Flickr, use the advanced search option and click on "Only search within Creative Common-licensed content." Using photos in worship or on your

bulletin cover that are copyrighted is not appropriate for a community of faith. Using this search feature helps you to avoid this possibility.

Chapter 3: Do You See What I See? Images and Preaching

1. André Resner, professor of preaching and worship at Hood Theological Seminary in Salisbury, North Carolina, has been helpful to me in referring to stories as "concretizations." He describes stories and images as needing to make real—concrete—your message. The more concrete the images are in the minds of the listeners, the better they can grasp them.

2. Richard A. Jensen, *Envisioning the Word: The Use of Visual Images in Preaching* (Minneapolis: Fortress Press, 2005), 17–24.

3. Ibid., 50–59.

4. Joel W. Martin and Conrad E. Oswalt, Jr., eds., *Screening the Sacred: Religion, Myth, and Ideology in Popular American Film* (San Francisco: Oxford Press, 1995), 153.

5. Jason Moore and Len Wilson, *Design Matters: Creating Powerful Imagery for Worship* (Nashville: Abingdon Press, 2006), 13.

6. Thomas H. Troeger, *Ten Strategies for Preaching in a MultiMedia Culture* (Nashville: Abingdon Press, 1996), 40.

7. Graham Johnston, *Preaching to a Postmodern World: A Guide to Reaching Twenty-First Century Listeners* (Grand Rapids: Baker Books, 2001), 159.

8. Luke 13:1–8.

9. These are items preachers should keep around them—either at their writing desk or someplace where they have easy access to them. Especially during back to school time, you can pick up boxes of crayons for under a dollar each. I often buy several boxes and keep them for clergy gatherings, classes, and meetings that I am leading.

Chapter 4: To Tweet or Not to Tweet: Social Media and Preaching

1. Joseph M. Webb, "Without Notes" in *New Interpreter's Handbook of Preaching* (Nashville: Abingdon Press, 2008), 429–30.

2. Ibid., 429–30.

3. Leonard I. Sweet, *Postmodern Pilgrims: First-Century Passion for the 21st Century Church (*Nashville: Broad & Holman Books, 2000).

4. Making things "real" is a hard concept to nail down, but many people today use this phrase. For the purposes of this book, I define it as creating opportunities to feel God's presence, love, and acceptance in ways that may be more relevant and profound than the normative experiences persons may have had in worship and preaching before.

5. Lucy Atkinson Rose, *Sharing the Word: Preaching in the Roundtable Church* (Louisville: Westminster John Knox Press, 1997), 33.

6. A difficult distinction due to the power dynamics of the preacher-parishioner relationship, but the tone of "speaking to" is often thought to be more instructional, academic, and theological in nature, while "speaking with" is often described as having a tone of collegiality, conversationally, and connection and is more related to narrative preaching than others.

7. Pew Research Study. "Why Americans Use Social Media" http://www.pewinternet.org/Reports/2011/Why-Americans-Use-Social-Media.aspx.

8. Ibid.

9. Ibid., 9.

10. Ibid.

11. Crowd sourcing is not a new phenomenon. Some have used pericope groups or lectionary-based Bible study groups as sources for preaching ideas. The idea of utilizing social media to further the reach and number of persons in the conversation can be quite helpful. Some pastors use Twitter or Facebook posts from either their personal pages or from congregational accounts. Others use email groups or even paper comment cards. There are many of options and possibilities for this activity. The point is to get people to be part of the pre- or post-sermon conversation.

12. Twitter hashtags are words or phrases preceded by a #, which allows persons to follow a particular topic by placing that hashtag in their own posts and/or searching for others who are posting the same hashtag. Virtually any group can create a hashtag and use it, but trying it out first to see if other groups are using that hashtag can be important. During a sermon, preachers can have their Twitter account open on their smart phone, laptop, or iPad to follow that specific hashtag or they could have a moderator preview them to place them up on a screen for all to see. There are also other resources, such as www.polleverywhere.com, that can allow you to create a unique feed for both texts and tweets to come into a common site for congregational viewing and for the pastor's own use.

13. Bonnie Rochman, "Twittering in Church, with the Pastor's OK," *Time* (May 3, 2009).

14. Mark 2:1–12.

15. Rochman, "Twittering in Church, with the Pastor's OK."

16. Ibid.

17. Adam Thomas, *Digital Disciple* (Nashville: Abingdon Press, 2011), chapter 3.

18. Dwight J. Friesen, *Thy Kingdom Connected: What the Church Can Learn from Facebook, the Internet, and Other Networks* (Grand Rapids: Baker Books, 2009), 64ff.

19. Lucy Atkinson Rose, *Sharing the Word: Preaching in the Roundtable Church.* (Louisville: Westminster John Knox Press, 1997).

20. Dan Kimball, *Thy Emerging Church: Vintage Christianity for New Generations* (Grand Rapids: Zondervan/emergentYS, 2003).

21. *Religion among the Millennials: Less Religiously Active Than Older Americans, but Fairly Traditional In Other Ways,* The PEW Forum on Religion and Public Life, February 17, 2010, http://pewforum.org/Age/Religion-Among-the-Millennials.aspx#attendance. While many studies bring this dissatisfaction to life, my dissertation research of over a hundred emerging churches and interviews and surveys done with members and leaders has allowed me to observe the disconnect as I have talked with younger persons. They believe the church does not meet their needs in many ways. They are most dissatisfied with how worship and preaching seem to be totally irrelevant and unconnected to their lives.

22. Leonard I. Sweet, *Viral: How Social Networking Is Poised to Ignite Revival* (Colorado Springs, Colo.: Waterbrook Press, 2012), 14.

23. HuffPo refers to the Huffington Post, which in an Internet news aggregator. These sites glean the Internet for the most interesting news and blogs or other syndicated web content and then they place them on their site in a central location under subheadings of interest to make surfing for a variety of topics more convenient. Other examples include *the Drudge Report* and *Google News.*

24. Sweet, *Virals,* 6.

25. I attended Saint Paul School of Theology in Kansas City, Missouri, from 1993 to 1996. During that time I took a number of courses with Dr. Townes. Remembering the exact date and course during which she shared this analogy is not possible. However, I owe a great debt to her for this tourist/pilgrim imagery. I have used it in teaching, preaching, and writing on several occasions.

26. Thomas, *Digital Disciple,* chapter 5.

27. Bob Rognlien, *Experiential Worship: Encountering God with Heart, Soul, Mind and Strength* (Colorado Springs, Colo.: Nav Press, 2005), 23.

28. Ibid., 30.

29. Kim Miller, *Designing Worship: Creating and Integrating Powerful God Experiences* (Loveland, Colo.: Group Publishing, 2004), 7.

Chapter 5: Screens in Worship: "Over My Dead Body!" or "Let's Do It!"

1. Leonard I. Sweet's Facebook status, August 10, 2012.

2. Tom Eason, *Media Ministry Made Easy: A Practical Guide to Visual Communication* (Nashville: Abingdon Press, 2003), 34. Most technicians and worship tech teams will agree that rear-projecting systems produce much more vibrant images. However, many sanctuaries do not allow for rear projecting so the decision for many is already made due to the logistics of the room.

3. Ibid., 62–63.

4. http://www.littlemountainproductions.com/ipodium/home.html.

Bibliography
(with additional resources)

Baker, Jonny, and Doug Gay with Jenny Brown. *Alternative Worship: Resources from and for the Emerging Church.* Grand Rapids: Baker Books, 2003.

Basden, Paul. *The Worship Maze: Finding a Style to Fit Your Church.* Downers Grove, Ill.: Intervarsity Press, 1999.

Borschel, Audrey. *Preaching Prophetically When the News Disturbs: Interpreting the Media.* St. Louis: Chalice Press, 2009.

Cameron, Julia. *The Artist's Way: A Spiritual Path to Higher Creativity.* New York: G. Putnam's Sons, 1992.

Cargal, Timothy B. *Hearing a Film, Seeing a Sermon: Preaching and Popular Movies.* Louisville: Westminster John Knox Press, 2007.

Carson, Timothy L. *Transforming Worship.* St. Louis: Chalice Press, 2003.

Dearborn, Tim A., and Scott Coil, eds. *Worship at the Next Level: Insight from Contemporary Voices.* Grand Rapids: Baker Books, 2004.

Eason, Tim. *Media Ministry Made Easy: A Practical Guide to Visual Communication.* Nashville: Abingdon Press, 2003.

Elkins, Heather Murray. "Altar-ing the World: Community-forming Word and Worship." In *Preaching in the Context of Worship*, David M. Greenhaw and Ronald J. Allen, eds. St. Louis: Chalice Press, 2000.

Foskett, Mary F., and O. Wesley Allen. *Interpreting the Bible: Approaching the Text in Preparation for Preaching Elements of Preaching.* Minneapolis: Fortress Press, 2009.

Friesen, Dwight J. *Thy Kingdom Connected: What the Church Can Learn from Facebook, the Internet, and Other Networks.* Grand Rapids: Baker Books, 2009.

Gibson, Scott M., ed. *Preaching to a Shifting Culture: 12 Perspectives on Communicating That Connects.* Grand Rapids: Baker Books, 2004.

Holbert, John C., and Alyce M. McKenzie. *What Not to Say: Avoiding the Common Mistakes That Can Sink Your Sermon.* Louisville: Westminster John Knox Press, 2011.

Jensen, Richard A. *Envisioning the Word: The Use of Visual Images in Preaching.* Minneapolis: Fortress Press, 2005.

Johnston, Graham. *Preaching to a Postmodern World: A Guide to Reaching Twenty-First Century Listeners.* Grand Rapids: Baker Books, 2001.